Words Aptly Spoken®
CHILDREN'S LITERATURE
an introduction to literary classics

THIRD EDITION

compiled and edited by Jen Greenholt

MULTIMEDIA

Jen Greenholt, *Words Aptly Spoken*® Series
An Introduction to Literary Classics, Children's Literature

Published by Classical Conversations® MultiMedia
255 Air Tool Drive
Southern Pines, NC 28387

CLASSICALCONVERSATIONS.COM
CLASSICALCONVERSATIONSBOOKS.COM

Cover design by Classical Conversations. Cover image from Library of Congress Cabinet of American Illustration collection: "Dick" by artist Thomas Fogarty, published ca. 1910.

ISBN: 978-0-9996995-6-0

Acknowledgments

Many thanks to the editors, tutors, and managers of Classical Conversations®, whose thoughts, input, and advice have gone into the creation of this book and whose support have made it possible; and to the many talented authors whose works I have been privileged to enjoy during the creation of this book.

Foreword

Learning to read is one of the most defining moments in life. It opens an unparalleled number of doors and possibilities, some of them life-changing. The books you read from that moment on have an enormous amount of power to shape your life. This is one of the characteristics that make quality children's literature so priceless.

Words Aptly Spoken®: Children's Literature takes you into the world of award-winning children's and young adult authors. Many of the books in this collection have won the Newbery Medal, one of the most prestigious awards for American children's literature. But while these books were first and foremost written for the enjoyment and education of children, they are not only for children. The lessons they teach and the courage of the people whose stories they tell are ageless. Everyone can take something away from these books, whether it is a better understanding of responsibility and selflessness or a new appreciation for the ability to read.

As with previous collections in the *Words Aptly Spoken* series, *Children's Literature* contains a series of questions about each work being studied. Review Questions ensure that you understand the basic plot, characters, setting, and message of the book. Thought Questions take the themes and ideas raised by each author and help you apply them to other, more familiar situations.

Children's Literature also introduces strategies for summarizing, creating chronologies and character charts, taking notes, and analyzing symbolism. Each of these skills will make reading and writing about classic literature a more fulfilling experience.

All this being said, take a deep breath and get ready to plunge into some great works of children's literature.

Table of Contents

A Note for Parents: Tools for the Journey

If you have ever heard Shakespeare performed before a live audience and marveled at the ease with which the words flowed from the actors' lips; if you have ever envied people who can call on Milton, Dickens, Joyce, and Lewis to lend eloquence to their argument; if you have skimmed a list of the hundred greatest novels of all time and winced as you remembered struggling to finish *The Grapes of Wrath* in high school—you may think that the great conversations of literature are forever closed to you.

The good news is, they're not! Whether you are a student, an adult, a parent, a child, or all of the above, you have the capability to train yourself not only to read great literature but also to share its beauty, truth, and joy with others.

Although most people learn to read as children, the art of deliberately engaging with the content and ideas of a novel or short story requires ongoing practice.

The *Words Aptly Spoken*® series is based on the classical model of education,[1] which breaks learning into three natural stages: grammar, dialectic, and rhetoric. In the grammar stage, you learn the vocabulary of a subject. In the dialectic stage, you learn to develop logical arguments and analyze others' ideas. In the rhetoric stage, you explore the consequences of ideas as you form and express your own. This guide will help you as you begin to apply the classical model to the study of literature.

Why Children's Literature?

As a parent or adult, you might be asking, "But why children's literature? Isn't that book too easy for my/my child's reading level?" First, consider a different question: Why do adults read aloud to small children, and then teach children to read using the same books? After all, they already know the endings!

That is precisely the point. Because children have heard the story many times, they can learn to identify the words on the page. Through repetition, they are able to focus on mastering a new skill without the distraction of unfamiliar content. The same is true as you train yourself to read great literature. Beginning with simple, familiar stories allows you to focus on the writer's craft.

How to Use This Book

Despite popular belief, reading is not wholly instinctive. Because comprehension, analysis, and critical thinking require practice, each work of literature you will study is broken down by chapter into a series of questions designed to give structure and guidance to your reading.

Although the questions are arranged chapter-by-chapter, most readers will not pause to answer questions after finishing a chapter. If the book has captured your imagination the way classic literature ought to, you won't want to stop reading! For this reason, treat these questions as tools not only for reading but also for writing, leading discussion, and sharing your ideas with others.

---

[1] See Dorothy Sayers' essay, "The Lost Tools of Learning."

Review Questions pull out the grammar for each chapter: Who is the book about? (Characters) What happens? (Plot) Where does it take place? (Setting) What is the message? (Theme) What is the scope or time frame? (Focus) For readers of all ages, repeatedly asking these questions will generate good reading habits; eventually, as you read, your brain will automatically take note of this information and store it for future use.

Thought Questions are an exercise in dialectic, taking the basic elements from the Review Questions and encouraging you to analyze that information in light of other knowledge. As you become more familiar with the building blocks of a story, you should begin to ask questions of your own. What does this mean for me? How should I respond to this argument? You can use the Thought Questions as a jump-start for your own thinking process, as training tools for leading discussion, or as topics for essays.

If you cannot answer some of the questions by the time you have finished the book, consider going back and reading over sections that you may only have skimmed the first time. A word of caution: don't merely "look up" the answers to the questions and skim the rest of the book. Once established, this habit will make it harder for you to read and understand more difficult books. After all, self-respecting Olympic runners know that they would be at a severe disadvantage in the actual games if they secretly completed only half of their daily training regimen. In the same way, the results you achieve as a reader will reflect the quality and consistency of your training.

Because measuring progress is a part of learning, each section in this book begins or ends with suggested reading and writing exercises that allow you to gauge how well you have mastered the skills you've been practicing. Completing every type of exercise for every book you read can make it harder to retain what you've learned. Parents with younger children may want to focus on the suggested Reading Practice exercise, while older children may gain more from Going Deeper. Although a particular exercise is suggested for each book studied, if you would rather practice a different skill or work on several skills at once, feel free to do so.

It is best if you have your own copy of each book so you can highlight or make notes in the margins. If, however, you need to use a copy belonging to the library or to a friend, consider reading with a small notebook or a pad of sticky notes nearby so you can jot down ideas and connections while they are fresh in your head.

The Journey in Perspective

One of the most important things to remember as you start—or resume—this journey is that it doesn't happen overnight. The art of leading and sharing in conversations about classical literature takes a lifetime to refine. You must begin with the fundamentals: learning to read closely, taking notes, and developing the vocabulary to structure your ideas and explain them to others (grammar). You must practice: adding new techniques, revising old ones, and comparing the results (dialectic). And then you will be ready to start all over again as you share the joy of the journey with others around you (rhetoric). Let's get started!

Reading Practice

Reading a science fiction novel and reading a textbook or an instruction manual might seem worlds apart, just as reading a short story might seem fundamentally unrelated to taking a test, interacting with strangers, or working in an office; however, all of these tasks require some of the same basic reading and writing skills. This section will introduce some of the skills that will equip you for reading- and writing-based tasks in any context.

Note-taking

One of the broadest reading skills is taking notes. The first thing to remember is that note-taking is not about copying what the book (or speaker) says word for word. Instead, it is about picking the most important information and putting it into your own words. A good test is to take notes only after you have stopped reading and set the book aside. To practice taking notes, read a paragraph or two, set down the book, and write a few words to remind you of the main ideas.

Keep in mind that notes do not have to be in full sentences. Unlike chapter summaries, notes do not simply record the plot; they may also include examples of symbolism, important quotes, key descriptions, recurring themes, or even hints about events to come. You can use anything from note cards to a blank piece of paper or sticky notes to record your ideas.

If you learn to take good notes from the books you read, not only will you have an easier time taking notes as you listen to a teacher's lecture but you will also have an easier time avoiding unintentional plagiarism. Plagiarism means taking someone else's words and using them as your own without giving credit to the author. (To avoid plagiarizing, place quotation marks around exact quotes, and be careful that your notes change more than a few words from the original.)

Note-taking is also a valuable skill outside of academics. A secretary recording the "minutes" of a meeting is taking notes. A lawyer listening to testimony and preparing for cross-examination and a doctor recording a patient's symptoms also need to be able to take good notes.

Chapter Summaries

A more specific type of note-taking is writing chapter summaries. After you finish reading each chapter, pause and set the book aside to think back over what happened. If necessary, re-read to refresh your memory. Then jot down the major events or points from the chapter. DO NOT write a chapter summary while looking at the book. If you need to look at the book in order to summarize what you have read, you should probably go back and read it again before you continue.

A chapter summary should be written in full sentences, and should be no longer than one paragraph (4–5 sentences). Essentially, a chapter summary is a tool you can use to remember what you have read so far. In an academic setting, chapter summaries are very helpful when you are looking for quotations to write a paper or studying for a test. This skill will be particularly valuable when you read books with long or complex chapters, including textbooks and nonfiction.

What is more, the ability to record and outline a sequence of events will help you write lab reports in the sciences, keep a journal when you go on an exciting trip, or even keep track of the strange noises your car is making so you can tell your mechanic.

Character Charts

Most books you read will have at least three or four characters in addition to the protagonist (main character). Some books have so many characters that it is difficult to keep them all straight! One tool that may help is a character chart. A character chart is simply a list of the people you encounter in the book, with a few brief notes or arrows indicating relationships between the characters. You can also write comments about the characters' personality traits, appearances, or choices. Include the page number with important points if possible.

When you read, keep your character chart nearby, so you can add notes and refer to it as you go. Then, if you have a question about how two characters are related, you won't have to search through the book to find the page where the characters were introduced. A character chart may also help you write essays, especially character sketches or book reports.

Creating character charts may seem like a task you would never use outside of school, but it teaches you a valuable skill. Substitute the word "person" for "character." Now imagine you are a diplomat. You are about to meet with three world leaders, and you need to know who they are and what makes them tick. How do you find out? You read their interviews. You read biographies and news stories about them. You take notes on their friendships, their enemies, and their likes and dislikes. You study their personality traits and choices. With all of this information, you are prepared when you enter the meeting.

On a smaller scale, think of a situation in which you might encounter strangers. Whether it's an interview with one person, a class with thirty, or a convention with a hundred, you want to be able to remember the names of people you meet and how they connect to each other and to you. Keeping track of the characters in a novel is a great way to practice.

Chronologies

Some books include flashbacks to earlier events or have two sequences of events going at the same time. A timeline allows you to see the events of the book as they occur in chronological order. Depending on the book's time span (a year, a month, a day), you may want to divide the timeline by larger or smaller increments of time (years, days, hours). If you are a visual learner, you can draw arrows from earlier events to the later events they influence.

As you prepare your timeline, think about whether some chapters have more action than others. Are there gaps in your timeline? What fills those gaps? Answering these questions will reveal places where the pace of the book slows down or speeds up. What important developments or themes appear in the slow parts? Are they important to the book's conclusion or larger message?

Although all of these considerations will help you write essays, in other situations, the skills you develop could also enable you analyze the development of a historical problem, unravel the events surrounding a crime, or create an itinerary for a group of people with busy schedules.

Maps

What chronologies do for time, maps do for space: they allow you to visualize the physical setting of a book. That is one reason many fantasy novels have a map on the inside cover or in the appendices. Because fantasy novels are set in a world that the author of the book has invented, authors and publishers realize that readers may need a map to bring the fantasy world to life.

Even though you may know the approximate geography of the United States or Europe or Africa, a map can still be a helpful tool to use as you read novels set in our world. For example, if you are reading a book about a military campaign, you may want to draw a map with the locations of major battles and colored lines to represent troop movements.

When you read a fantasy novel, use the author's descriptions to create your own map. If the book already has one, consider making a copy so you can add your own details. If the book is set in the real world, use an atlas to copy the basic shape of the country or state, and then add details mentioned in the book. Write down place names and major events that happen at each location. If you have space, jot down some of the important historical features of each location. If the main characters go on a journey, mark their route with colored pencils. (For a good example, look at the maps accompanying J.R.R. Tolkien's *The Hobbit* or *The Lord of the Rings*).

Not only will map-making improve your knowledge of geography; it will also make you more aware of the way that landscape can affect events. When Hitler's troops invaded the Soviet Union in 1941, they underestimated both the distance their supply lines would have to stretch and the fierceness of Soviet winters. The western prairies and the mountains of Colorado will present different challenges to the characters and real people who live in those places.

Glossaries of Terms

Reading is one of the most important ways to expand your vocabulary. Some of the process is unconscious. You learn what a word means by its context. The next time you see the word you modify or confirm your original assumption based on the new context. However, deliberate practice will give you greater speed and accuracy as you learn new words, especially those for which context may not provide the meaning right away.

Some books use technical terms (science fiction), local slang (*The Adventures of Tom Sawyer* is a good example), or made-up words (fantasy novels). Some authors also use big or old-fashioned words that you may not recognize. Shakespeare is notoriously difficult for new readers, in part because everyday English in 1600 was very different from the English you hear today. In addition, writers from England, South Africa, New Zealand, or even New York, may use words that are specific to their culture and not widely known in other places.

If you come across an unfamiliar word, take a minute to write it down, along with a brief definition. That way if you see the word again, you can refer back to your glossary. The repetition of reading a word, then writing it, then looking at it will implant the word more firmly in your mind and increase the likelihood that you will remember it the next time you need it.

Going Deeper

One of the most exciting things about classic literature is the layers of meaning and ideas. On the surface, a book may be enjoyable to read because it has good action and interesting characters. If you read it again, you might begin to see parallels in the way two characters deal with their problems. A third reading might lead you to ponder a similar struggle in your own life, and a fourth might challenge you to respond to your problem in a different way.

Authors use a variety of tools to create these layers. This section will explore some common methods and give you the tools to reach a deeper understanding of your favorite books and a deeper appreciation for any book you encounter.

Genre

A *genre* is a category of literature based on the books' shared style, theme, or form. (*Genre* is a French word meaning "a kind or type of thing," and it comes from the Latin word *genus*.) Although all of the books in this study guide can be loosely classified as children's literature, each one is slightly different.

Some of these books are historical fiction: stories set in real places and times in the past, but about fictional characters (*The Door in the Wall*). Some are realistic fiction: stories set in or near the author's own time period (*Where the Red Fern Grows*). Some are biographies: stories based on the lives of real people, either in their own words (*The Hiding Place*) or as told by others (*Amos Fortune, Free Man*). Others are fantasy: books set in worlds that are completely imaginary (*The Phantom Tollbooth*) or a combination of imaginary and real (*The Magician's Nephew*). Some books are difficult to classify because they include elements of several different genres.

When you read books from different genres, you will need to bring with you a different set of expectations. Just as your expectations vary when reading a user manual or a newspaper, literary genres may influence the way you understand a particular book. You might approach a fantasy novel knowing that some of the characters or situations could not occur in the real world. A work of historical fiction might have been limited by the author's access to research materials. Whereas in a work of fiction, an author might use the weather to suggest the mood of a scene, in a biography, a thunderstorm could simply be a factual detail from actual records.

Certain genres are better suited to giving a moral lesson, while others stir your imagination or teach you about history. As you read, think about the genre of each book from an author's perspective. Ask yourself what challenges and opportunities that genre presents to a writer. Always take genre into account when you analyze a book's purpose or claim to truth.

Themes

In the classic British novel *Frankenstein* by Mary Shelley, the main plot is about a scientist, Victor Frankenstein, who is so determined to pursue the possibilities of science that he neglects the ethical consequences of his actions. Most of the action is recorded, however, in a series of letters written by a minor character, explorer Robert Walton, who is bent on reaching the North Pole. His blind determination, without regard to the consequences, leads him into grave danger, where he meets Frankenstein. Do you sense a pattern?

Authors sometimes use minor events, characters, or problems (sub-plots), to reflect or emphasize the main plot. For example, if the central conflict of the book is caused by a character's selfishness, then the story might open with an argument between that character and his sibling over his unwillingness to share. Alternately, as in *Frankenstein*, one character— Frankenstein—might serve as a mirror in which another character—Walton—sees his flaws magnified. Parallels can also appear across generations (a son develops the same faults as his father) or cultural and economic situations. *The Prince and the Pauper*, by Mark Twain, is a famous example of the latter.

As you read, be on the lookout for characters who share a common fear, flaw, or personality trait. Ask yourself what the situation confronting the main character has in common with the minor characters' circumstances. Try to identify the main theme of the book, and then look for ways that each character or situation relates to that theme. If there is a character or sub-plot that seems totally out of place, think about ways it might illustrate the theme by showing its opposite.

Character Development

At the beginning of Esther Forbes's award-winning American novel *Johnny Tremain*, Johnny is a self-serving, arrogant young man who views other people as stepping stones to his own ends. By the end of the novel, he has become not only humble but also self-sacrificing for the sake of a greater cause. His transformation is what drives the plot and makes the story compelling.

If the main characters in a novel never changed, the novel itself would be much less interesting to read. Because humans are complicated and unpredictable, it is easier to identify with a character who shares those traits. For this reason, one way "classic" literature has been defined is that it contains characters who are complex and who grow or change over the course of the book. Change is not instantaneous, and authors use encounters, mishaps, and other characters to demonstrate the main character's growth.

After you finish reading, go back and look at the main character's first words at the beginning of the book. Look at the words the author uses to describe him or her. Now look at the character's last words, and the last description. What differences do you see? Think about the events and relationships that produced a noticeable change or caused the character to reevaluate his life, and use this information to identify the major turning points in the character's development.

Imagery

One of the most difficult jobs for a filmmaker is to turn a well-known book into a movie. Why? Because so many people have mental images of the settings and characters in the book, and everyone has a different idea of how their favorite scene should look.

In a film or play, the director can use physical props, sets, and costumes to show you her vision for a scene. In a book, the author must use words instead. Some descriptions are fairly straightforward: she wore a long, blue dress; three oak trees lined the driveway; it was July in New York City. Other descriptions are more subjective: the house was gloomy and vaguely threatening; the street was like a Baroque painting.

When you read a particularly vivid passage in a book, take a minute to sketch the scene. Compare your drawing with another person who has read the same book. Try to figure out why the drawings are different. If possible, look at an illustrated copy of the book, and see how close your vision of the scene comes to that of the illustrator. Think about the ability of certain words to produce a particular emotion. How did the author use these words to create a picture in your mind? When you write, think about ways you can use word choice to convey a certain mood.

Symbolism

When is a tree not a tree? Trick question, right? Not necessarily. In literature, sometimes a simple object or action represents something much larger. For example, in E.G. Speare's *The Bronze Bow*, the sandals Daniel must wear when he returns to the village and the cleansing rituals he must follow are symbolic of the constraint he feels when he is in the village.

Sometimes the symbol is not a specific object, but rather a pattern of events or ideas repeated on small and large scales. In *The Hiding Place*, Corrie ten Boom identifies symbolism in her own life. When Father does not let Corrie carry his briefcase because it is too heavy for her, she reflects that this is similar to the way in which God sometimes denies humans full knowledge because He knows they are not strong enough to bear it.

As you read, be on the lookout for symbolism. Authors rarely include details or describe a scene in a certain way without a purpose. Try to think how small events and interactions reflect the larger lessons of the book. And even though the "dark and stormy night" with which the cartoon character Snoopy began his novels is a bit overdramatic, keep in mind that something as simple as a rainstorm or planting a tree may reflect a transition in the book or in the life of a character.

Worldview

Have you ever stopped to consider why wearing a hat in church is frowned upon? Why "boys don't cry"? Why it is impolite to ask someone how much money they make? These and many other assumptions are part of our culture, part of the invisible rulebook that influences how we choose to behave. We act according to similar assumptions every day, often without recognizing that we are following "rules" at all.

In the same way, books present you with worlds in which certain things are taken for granted. If you read a book written or set during the Civil War, most likely the female characters will wear dresses and perhaps corsets. Owning slaves may be acceptable. The characters will not question these things, and you may not be expected to question them either.

On one hand, this is the mark of a well-written book set outside the reader's place and time. The author needs you to accept the characters' world (with all its peculiarities) as a place as normal as your own world. It can be easy to get swept up in the author's view of the universe, to blindly accept the philosophies, worldview, and actions of the characters without questioning. Being carried away by the author's imagination is one of the great joys of reading. But at the same time, it is wise to be aware of the book's subtler messages.

Every author has been influenced by his or her time. As a result, he may take for granted some things that you would never accept or believe. Paying attention to the author's deliberate or unconscious assumptions not only will make you a better reader, it will also challenge you to recognize and analyze your own culture's version of "normal."

When you read, ask yourself these questions: what do the characters assume about the way the world works? What are the book's assumptions about religion? Human nature? Gender? Families? The natural world? Do the consequences of the characters' actions (or lack thereof) encourage you to follow their example?

Some details are simply different and provide a window into a historical period or fantasy world. However, some books may imply that it is okay to disregard morals "under [fill-in-the-blank] circumstances" or that "obviously [fill-in-the-blank] is true around the world." Both can provide excellent topics for discussion—if you're paying attention. So when you read, enjoy the details that make living on Mars or in the nineteenth century seem equally possible, but don't get so caught up in the music that you miss the lyrics.

Remember, there is a difference between blindly absorbing a book's messages and wisely considering them in light of truth. It is important to acknowledge that while the great classical conversations of world literature will inspire you, they will also challenge you. If you can approach them with a spirit of thoughtful critique rather than fear, you will be able to celebrate the discovery of truth and beauty in literature with that much more joy.

The Magician's Nephew
C. S. Lewis

Introduction

Clive Staples Lewis (1898–1963) is one of the most prominent authors in twentieth-century Christian literature. After a personal investigation of Christianity, Lewis went on to write books on topics ranging from pain and loss to the meaning of biblical love. Lewis also wrote a number of Christian-themed children's and science fiction novels. *The Magician's Nephew* was published in 1955. It is the prequel to Lewis' famed *Chronicles of Narnia* series, although it was written later than most of the other books. *The Magician's Nephew* introduces readers to the world of Narnia and sets the stage for the next book, *The Lion, the Witch and the Wardrobe*.

Reading Practice: Maps

Look at several different types of maps: road maps, topographic maps, political maps, physical maps, climate maps, and resource or economic maps. Which types might be relevant or helpful for this book? Draw maps of the Wood Between the Worlds, Charn, and Narnia. Try to include as many details from the text as you can.

Going Deeper: Worldview

In this book, you will be introduced to several philosophies of "proper" human behavior. Try to identify the basic principles by which characters live. Compare and contrast the worldviews of Uncle Andrew, Jadis, and Aslan. Identify their highest values, the rules they refuse to break, and their priorities. Then ask yourself if the differences help to explain the conflict between them.

Another part of worldview in *The Chronicles of Narnia* that might spark conversation is the presence of magic. *The Magician's Nephew* contains references to three very different types of magic: Uncle Andrew's, Jadis's, and Aslan's. As you read, think about the way Lewis portrays magic. Does it have a clear source? Is it good, evil, or neutral? For parents, this is a great opportunity to respond not with fear but with wisdom as you discuss these questions with your children. For students, it's a chance to think critically about the possibilities and challenges of using fiction—especially fantasy—to communicate truth.

Chapter 1

Review Questions
1. How did Polly and Digory meet?
2. Why was Digory unhappy?
3. Which house did Polly and Digory enter from the tunnel?
4. What was the humming noise that Polly heard?
5. What did Uncle Andrew want to give Polly? What happened when Polly took the gift?

Thought Questions
1. How did Polly and Digory become friends? Were they very similar? How were they different? How do you make friends? Which is more important, similarity or being in a situation in which you need the other person?
2. Why did Polly accept Uncle Andrew's gift? How did he persuade her? Do you think you would have been fooled by his persuasion?

Chapter 2

Review Questions
1. Who was Mrs. Lefay? What was unusual about her?
2. Where had Mrs. Lefay gotten her box?
3. What was the difference between the yellow and green rings?
4. Why didn't Uncle Andrew want to go to the Other Place?
5. How did Uncle Andrew convince Digory to take the ring?

Thought Questions
1. Uncle Andrew says that promises and rules only apply to little boys, servants, and women. What does this tell you about his views on children? Women? Servants?
2. Do you think someone should be free from moral rules if they are particularly smart or powerful?
3. Do superheroes obey the law? Are the results of their actions generally good or bad?
4. Do you think Uncle Andrew was a coward? Explain.
5. Before he leaves, Digory says he "could not decently have done anything else." Do you agree? Why or why not?

Chapter 3

Review Questions
1. Where did Digory go when he put on the yellow ring?
2. How did Digory describe the Wood?
3. Whom did Digory meet beside the pool?
4. What prevented Polly and Digory from going straight home?
5. What did Digory almost forget to do (just before they set out to explore)?
6. Why didn't the yellow rings take Polly and Digory into another world?

Thought Questions
1. How would you decide what kind of scientific tests are ethical (for example, using human volunteers, testing on yourself, or using animals)?
2. How had Uncle Andrew misunderstood the function of the rings? Why do you think he made that mistake? Is it wise to use something you don't understand completely?

Chapter 4

Review Questions
1. Describe the new world Digory and Polly entered.
2. How did Polly and Digory know this new world was very old?
3. What did the children see in the great hall?
4. How did the faces change as the children went farther into the room?
5. Did Polly want to strike the bell? Why or why not? Did Digory? Why?
6. What happened when the bell was struck?

Thought Questions
1. Digory describes the last woman in the hall as both very beautiful and very cruel. Is this possible? Does physical beauty have anything to do with goodness?
2. What do you think the poem on the pillar means?
3. Would you have struck the bell? Why or why not?
4. Is curiosity a bad thing? When does it become dangerous or harmful?

Chapter 5

Review Questions
1. How did the Queen, Polly, and Digory get through the doors?
2. Who destroyed Charn? How was it destroyed? Why was it destroyed?
3. How did Polly and Digory escape Charn? What went wrong with their escape?

Thought Questions
1. What was Digory's view of the Queen? Polly's? Why do you think the two children saw the Queen differently? In your opinion, who was right? Why?
2. How are the Queen and Uncle Andrew similar? How are they different? Which one is more dangerous? Is that a distinction you can make?

Chapter 6

Review Questions
1. What did the trip back to the Wood teach the children about the rings?
2. What did Polly want to do to Jadis in the Wood between the Worlds?
3. How did Jadis get to London?
4. What did the narrator describe as "Uncle Andrew's silliness"?

Thought Questions
1. Do you agree with Polly that she and Digory would have been justified in leaving the Queen in the Wood?
2. What do you think is the mark of a magician?
3. If you did wicked things over and over again, would it change your appearance? Why or why not? If so, how?
4. Look back at Chapter 4 (Thought Questions): what common theme do you see?

Chapter 7

Review Questions
1. Why couldn't Polly go back to help Digory?
2. How did Digory plan to get rid of the Witch?
3. Why did Digory suddenly want to go back to the Wood? What prevented him?

Thought Questions

4. Would it have been wrong for Digory to leave Jadis in London? Was she his responsibility? What is the difference between a problem that is your fault and one that is your responsibility?

Chapter 8

Review Questions

1. How many people did Digory bring with him to the Wood? Who were they?
2. Which world did the group enter by mistake?
3. What happened when the voice began to sing?
4. Who was the singer?

Thought Questions

1. If the music and singing were so beautiful, why do you think the Witch hated them?
2. Why do you think Lewis uses music instead of just words to create Narnia?
3. What is the most beautiful sound you have ever heard? What do you imagine the Lion's singing sounded like? What adjectives does Lewis use to describe it? What impression do the words convey?

Chapter 9

Review Questions

1. What happened when the Witch threw the iron bar at the Lion?
2. What did Uncle Andrew want to do with the new world?
3. Why did Polly compare Uncle Andrew to the Witch?
4. What did the Lion do to the animals he selected?

Thought Questions

1. Polly says everything in Narnia comes "out of the Lion's head." What does she mean? Do you agree?
2. What parallels can you find between this creation story and the one found in Genesis 1–2? What are some significant differences?
3. What is wrong with Uncle Andrew's plan for the new world?
4. Is it a good thing to use the resources around you? When does it become a bad thing?

Chapter 10

Review Questions

1. What was the first joke in Narnia?
2. Why couldn't Uncle Andrew hear Aslan talking?
3. Did Strawberry remember the Cabman?

Thought Questions

1. Have you ever tried to convince yourself that something unpleasant was untrue? If so, why? Did you begin to believe it?
2. Is it hard for you to admit when you're wrong? Why do you think people are afraid to be incorrect?
3. How do your preconceived ideas about other people impact the way you see and interact with them?

Chapter 11

Review Questions
1. What did the animals think of Uncle Andrew? What did they do to him?
2. What did Aslan say when Digory asked him for help?
3. How did the Cabby's wife get to Narnia?
4. What did Aslan say were the qualities a king should have?
5. Who were the first king and queen of Narnia?

Thought Questions
1. Compare the way the animals in Narnia view humans to the way you think about animals. Do you think this book claims that animals and humans are equal? If not, why not?
2. What is the risk in stereotyping (making assumptions about) people based on the way they look?
3. Do you think it was fair for Aslan to blame Digory for the Witch's coming to Narnia?
4. In your mind, what sets kings and queens apart from other people? What additional responsibilities should they have? What additional privileges?

Chapter 12

Review Questions
1. What did Aslan ask Digory to do?
2. What was Strawberry's new name? How did he get it?
3. Why did Digory and Polly bury the ninth toffee?
4. What did the children hear just as they were about to go to sleep?

Thought Questions
1. Why do you think Aslan had tears in his eyes when he talked about Digory's mother? How is this story similar to the one in John 11?
2. Why did Aslan say that only he and Digory know how powerful grief can be? Do you think he's right?
3. Fledge says although Aslan knows what the children need, he likes to be asked. Do you think the same thing is true of God? Why or why not?

Chapter 13

Review Questions
1. Why didn't Polly and Fledge go into the garden with Digory?
2. Why didn't Digory take one of the apples for himself?
3. Whom did Digory meet in the garden?
4. How did the Witch change after she ate the apple?
5. What strategy did the Witch use to persuade Digory to steal one of the apples?
6. What was the Witch's mistake?

Thought Questions
1. Digory asks, "Who would want to climb a wall if he could get in by a gate?" He thought the answer was obvious. Do you? What is the difference between climbing a wall and entering through a gate? Why might someone choose to climb the wall instead?
2. Did Digory owe Aslan anything, as the Witch asks? Why or why not?

Chapter 14

Review Questions
1. What did Aslan do with the apple Digory brought?
2. What was inside the animals' cage?
3. What happened to the apple? What was its purpose? Its power?
4. What did Aslan say would happen to the Witch because she had eaten an apple?
5. What gift did Aslan give Digory?

Thought Questions
1. Aslan says, "Oh, Adam's sons, how cleverly you defend yourselves against all that might do you good!" Explain. Can you think of an example of this in your own life?
2. Why could Aslan give Digory an apple if Digory was forbidden to take one?

Chapter 15

Review Questions
1. What was Aslan's warning? His command?
2. How long were the children and Uncle Andrew gone?
3. What effect, if any, did the apple have on Digory's mother?
4. What did Polly and Digory do with the rings and the apple core?
5. How was Digory's apple tree connected to the tree in Narnia?

Thought Questions
1. Why didn't the children need to use the rings when they were with Aslan?
2. Why did the apples have a different effect on the Witch and on Digory's mother?
3. What do you think ultimately caused Uncle Andrew to learn his lesson?
4. If you have already read *The Lion, the Witch and the Wardrobe*, how does Lewis set the stage for that book in the ending of *The Magician's Nephew*?

The Bronze Bow
Elizabeth George Speare

Introduction

Elizabeth George Speare (1908–1994) was a beloved American author of historical fiction for children. Speare won her first Newbery Medal in 1959 for her novel *The Witch of Blackbird Pond*, an account of the Salem witch trials. In 1962, she received a second Newbery award for *The Bronze Bow*, which was published in 1961. Set in first-century AD Galilee, *The Bronze Bow* explores themes of vengeance, forgiveness, and the meaning of God's victory.

Reading Practice: Chapter Summary

After you finish reading each chapter, pause and set the book aside to think back over what happened. Jot down the major events or points from the chapter. Remember to use full sentences, and write no more than one paragraph (4–5 sentences) per chapter.

Going Deeper: Character Development

Look at Daniel's first scene in *The Bronze Bow*. Then look at his final scene. Pay attention to the words Speare uses to describe Daniel. What do the differences between the two scenes suggest about Daniel's growth? Using your chapter summaries, think about the events and relationships that produced a noticeable change or caused him to reevaluate his life. Try to identify the major turning points in Daniel's character. Now do the same thing for Thacia and Joel.

Because *The Bronze Bow* is historical fiction, some of the characters are real people. As you read, think about the risks an author takes in writing fiction that includes real people. Pay particular attention to the way Speare depicts Jesus and His disciples. How closely does her dialogue match the accounts in the Bible? What characteristics does she emphasize? Discuss how her retelling of biblical stories might help you understand the originals better.

Chapter 1

Review Questions

1. What marked Daniel as a Galilean?
2. For whom was Daniel waiting? Why?
3. What message did Daniel wish to send, and to whom?
4. What did Joel and Thacia do before they ate? Why did it surprise Daniel?
5. Why had Daniel joined the robbers?
6. Why didn't Joel want to move to Capernaum?
7. How did Daniel view the Roman presence?
8. Who was Rosh?

Thought Questions

1. If you were away from home for five years, would you forget your old life? Is there a difference between moving on with your life and trying to escape your past?
2. What gives a slave or a bound person the right to run away? What standard would you use to answer that question?
3. Is freedom a natural right? Defend your answer, and remember to define your terms!
4. What causes your conscience to become dull or silent? Can you ever permanently quiet your conscience?
5. What is the difference between a bandit and a hero? Can a person be both?

Chapter 2

Review Questions

1. For what did Rosh need Daniel?
2. How did Daniel convince Joel to leave? What did Joel do instead?
3. What was Daniel's role in the plan?
4. What happened to Joel when he tried to help?
5. How did Joel respond to Rosh's threats?
6. Who took charge of the slave?
7. What did Samson do once he was free?

Thought Questions

1. If you are enslaved, does it matter who your master is? Why or why not? Was Samson truly free once Daniel removed his chains?
2. Why do you think it mattered to Rosh that Samson slept free?
3. Is it possible to get satisfaction from a life driven by violence? Explain. What would be missing from that kind of lifestyle?

Chapter 3

Review Questions

1. What made it difficult for Daniel to look after Samson?
2. Why did Daniel resent Samson?
3. Who came looking for Daniel? What news did he bring?
4. Why didn't Simon want to join Rosh?
5. Why did the two men need to bathe before entering the village?
6. What was the matter with Daniel's sister?
7. What was the "pauper's share"?
8. Where did Daniel's grandmother work? What did she do?

Thought Questions
1. Is it reasonable to disagree with someone's methods if you have the same goal? Explain.
2. Is it ever shameful to be poor? If so, when?
3. Why do you think Daniel felt threatened by Leah?
4. How did Daniel's character change to make him no longer feel at home in the village?

Chapter 4

Review Questions
1. Why did Simon want Daniel to go with him to the synagogue?
2. How did Daniel explain his sister's strange behavior?
3. What did Daniel hope Jesus would say?
4. Why had the people of Nazareth tried to kill Jesus?
5. What happened as Daniel was returning home?
6. In Daniel's eyes, how did Jesus and Rosh compare?

Thought Questions
1. Do you think Leah had a physical or a spiritual problem? Are the two always separate? Are there mental problems that science cannot explain? Discuss.
2. What is a *Zealot*? Do you think Jesus was a Zealot? Why or why not?
3. Answer Daniel's question: Where does the call of Jesus lead?
4. Why do you think Daniel left the village?

Chapter 5

Review Questions
1. Why did Daniel want to find Joel? What was Rosh's response?
2. Why did Daniel leave the place where Jesus was teaching?
3. How was Daniel welcomed at the house of Hezron?
4. What actions of the Hezron family did Daniel describe as "heathen"?
5. How did Daniel insult Rabbi Hezron?
6. What did Rabbi Hezron say in response to Daniel's accusations?
7. What was Israel's "one great strength" according to Rabbi Hezron?

Thought Questions
1. While Daniel was gone, did things change on the mountain? If not, why was he disillusioned when he returned?
2. Explain Rosh's statement about Joel: "He's got too much to lose." Why was he unlikely to join Rosh's band?
3. Do you think the Jews lost their pride if they were civil to the Roman soldiers?
4. Why do you think Malthace shrank back from Daniel? What does her response reveal about her character?
5. Did Hezron and Daniel react angrily to Joel's suggestion for the same reason? Explain.
6. Did Daniel view Romans collectively or as individuals? Was his judgment fair?
7. Was Rabbi Hezron right about Israel's "one great strength"? Discuss.

Chapter 6

Review Questions
1. What happened at the well?
2. Where did Daniel seek shelter?
3. What did Malthace tell Daniel to do?
4. How did Joel react when he found Daniel?
5. Where did Thace and Joel hide Daniel?

Thought Questions
1. Why do you think Thace rescued Daniel?
2. Was it selfish for Daniel to endanger the house of Hezron?
3. Do you think Rabbi Hezron would have turned Daniel over to the Romans?

Chapter 7

Review Questions
1. What did Rabbi Hezron believe about fighting? What did Joel believe? Daniel? Thace?
2. Why did Daniel hate the Romans?
3. What had Daniel vowed?
4. Why couldn't Thacia take Daniel and Joel's vow?
5. What was the new vow?
6. How did Thace explain the bronze bow?
7. Why did Daniel decide to leave?

Thought Questions
1. Do you think God uses outlaws? Do you think Rosh was doing God's work?
2. What did Joel mean when he said, "…it is the same thing. Victory and the kingdom"?
3. What made the new vow different from the one Daniel had originally taken?

Chapter 8

Review Questions
1. Who became Daniel's hero?
2. How did Thacia and Leah threaten Daniel's plans?
3. Why were the man and woman taking their son to see Jesus?
4. Why did Jesus say hand-washing was unnecessary?
5. For what reason did Daniel question the relevance of Jesus' words to the crowd?
6. What did Simon want of Jesus?

Thought Questions
1. Why were so many people curious about Jesus?
2. Why didn't the man and woman need to look at their son to know he had been healed?
3. Why do you think Joel stopped short of condemning Jesus?

Chapter 9

Review Questions
1. What job did Rosh give Daniel?
2. Why did Daniel give one of the daggers back to the man?

3. What did Rosh say when he found out?
4. What did Rosh tell Daniel he needed to do? Why?

Thought Questions
1. Does Rosh sound like Robin Hood to you? How are they alike? Different?
2. Do you think Rosh's actions were justifiable? Why or why not?
3. Is wealth a right or a privilege? Did the old man deserve to have his gold taken away?
4. Is kindness the same thing as weakness? Explain.

Chapter 10

Review Questions
1. What message did Simon send to Daniel?
2. Why had the villagers not entered the house?
3. What psalm did Daniel recite to his grandmother?
4. What sign told Daniel that his sister was not totally in the grip of the demons?
5. What happened to his grandmother?

Thought Questions
1. Why was Daniel afraid to spend the night in his grandmother's house? Was his fear reasonable? What does his reaction tell you about his view of death?
2. Why do you think Daniel's grandmother expected him to return?

Chapter 11

Review Questions
1. What did Simon offer Daniel?
2. What was the hardest part of the job for Daniel to accept?
3. How did Daniel get Leah to Simon's house?
4. What did Leah find to occupy her time while Daniel worked?
5. How did Daniel show his contempt for the soldier?
6. What did the soldier see? How did Daniel react?

Thought Questions
1. How did Simon differentiate between a villager and an outlaw? Do you agree with him?
2. Did it surprise you to learn that Leah was a skilled weaver? Why or why not? What assumptions do you make about people with mental disabilities?
3. Why do you think the incident with the soldier made Daniel long for the mountain?

Chapter 12

Review Questions
1. Why did Daniel speak to the village boy?
2. For what reason had the boy's friends attacked him?
3. How did Daniel help Nathan?
4. Whom did Joel bring to the shop?
5. What was the password of Daniel's band?
6. Why did the group need to change its meeting place?

Thought Questions
1. Does it shock you to think of a family selling their daughter? What modern social practices do you think would have shocked people in Daniel's time?
2. What is the purpose of a brand? Does it undermine the power of giving your word? How do people guarantee their promises today? Discuss in light of Matthew 5:33–37.

Chapter 13

Review Questions
1. What did Leah do with the coin she received for her weaving?
2. Why did Daniel ask Joel to speak to the young weaver?
3. Why did Joel go to hear Jesus speak?
4. What did the boys find when they returned to the house?
5. What did Daniel notice after Thacia's visit?
6. What made Leah laugh?

Thought Questions
1. Did Jesus and Rosh have anything in common? Would they have worked together? Why or why not?
2. Why do you think Leah allowed Thacia to see her?
3. In your opinion, what factors brought about the changes in Leah?

Chapter 14

Review Questions
1. What did Leah ask Daniel to explain?
2. What did Leah say about the soldier? How did she know?
3. What did Daniel find on the mountain?
4. Why did Rosh resent Samson?
5. Why couldn't Daniel take Samson back to the village with him?

Thought Questions
1. Why did Daniel think marriage was foolish? Do you think his reasons were valid?
2. What makes someone a master? Do they need the other person's consent?
3. Did Daniel belong in the village or on the mountain? Explain.

Chapter 15

Review Questions
1. Why did Daniel go to hear Jesus speak?
2. Why did the overseers object to Jesus?
3. What story did Leah like to hear? What puzzled Daniel about the story?
4. To what did Daniel attribute the changes in Leah?
5. What did Daniel make in his spare time?

Thought Questions
1. Why did it seem foolish to Daniel that a Jew and Samaritan could work together? Can you think of a comparable conflict between two groups of people today?
2. Is there a person or group of people with whom you could never get along? Is it easier to seek reconciliation or to say it's impossible?

3. Have you ever asked, "How long must the world go on like this?" What situation produced the question? What was your answer?

Chapter 16

Review Questions
1. What did Rosh want Joel to do?
2. How did Joel propose to get the information?
3. Why didn't Thacia want to see Jesus while she and Daniel were disguised?
4. What happened with the soldiers?
5. What did Thacia say to make Leah laugh?
6. What broke up the noon meal?
7. What did Daniel give Thacia?
8. What had the doctors said about Leah?

Thought Questions
1. Do you think Jesus would have condemned Thacia's actions? Support your answer.
2. Are all lies equally bad? Think carefully before you answer. What about a situation in which a lie could save an innocent person's life?
3. Why did Thacia admire Daniel's actions? In your opinion, were they wise? Brave?
4. What makes the world worth living in?

Chapter 17

Review Questions
1. What had Rosh done? How did the legionaries know he was responsible?
2. What role did Joel undertake for Rosh?
3. Why did Daniel's band join active service?
4. Why was Daniel disappointed in his boys?
5. What did the boys find on the road? How did the Romans respond to the theft?
6. What happened to make the townspeople lose patience with Rosh?
7. How did Rosh respond to Daniel's warning?

Thought Questions
1. Do you think Rosh's plan was worthy of Joel's efforts? What purpose did it serve?
2. Why do looting, vandalism, and theft often accompany war? Are these acts justifiable?
3. Was Rosh giving his life for the people's freedom? Explain.
4. Do you think Rosh's evaluation of the townspeople was fair? Why or why not?

Chapter 18

Review Questions
1. Who came to find Daniel? What news did he bring?
2. What did Rosh say they should do?
3. What did Daniel decide to do?
4. Who became the official leader of the band of boys?

Thought Questions
1. What caused Daniel to see Rosh differently? Did Rosh change, or did Daniel? Explain.

2. Is collective responsibility (being responsible for the members of a group) or individual responsibility (being responsible only for yourself) more important? In what situations would you be in favor of collective responsibility?

Chapter 19

Review Questions
1. Did Daniel expect to survive the attack? Why or why not?
2. What did the Romans do that threw Daniel off guard?
3. What unlooked-for help came to Daniel and the other boys?
4. How did the battle end?
5. What happened to Samson?
6. What did the boys lose that night?

Thought Questions
1. What was the difference between the fight and the glorious battle Daniel longed for?
2. Is war ever truly glorious? Why do you think people want to view it that way? Explain.
3. Was the fight worth the cost, in your opinion? Defend your position.
4. How might the fight have been avoided?
5. How would a captain in Daniel's position decide which man to lose? How would you decide? What does Daniel's decision reveal about his character?

Chapter 20

Review Questions
1. Describe a life that is lived by the sword.
2. Why did Joel come to see Daniel?
3. Why did Daniel no longer see Rosh as his leader?
4. What means did Daniel use to persuade Joel to continue his studies?
5. What message did Thacia send Daniel?
6. Why had Thacia not been forced to accept an arranged marriage?
7. Who were Jesus' enemies?

Thought Questions
1. Why is it easier to deceive someone who is angry at you? Is deception justifiable in that situation?
2. Why was Daniel angry to hear that Thacia refused to choose a husband?
3. Do you think people serving in the military should get married? Discuss.

Chapter 21

Review Questions
1. Why did the priests from Judea question Jesus?
2. Why did Daniel feel the need to speak to Jesus?
3. Who or what, according to Jesus, was the enemy?
4. Why couldn't Daniel follow Jesus? What did Jesus ask him to give up?
5. How did Jesus respond when he heard about Daniel's vow?

Thought Questions
1. Can freedom ever come from vengeance and hate? Explain.

2. What does it mean to repay love with hate? Is that what Daniel was trying to do? Is it possible to distinguish between justice and revenge? If so, how?
3. Do you think Daniel's was a vow of hate?
4. Do you treat vows as if they are sacred? Why or why not? Look back at Chapter 12 (Thought Questions). Do you see a theme?

Chapter 22

Review Questions
1. What set Daniel apart from the other young men at the wedding?
2. Why did Daniel leave the festival?
3. What was Leah's surprise at dinner? Where had she gotten it?
4. How did Leah know the Roman?
5. What did Daniel make her promise?
6. Why did Daniel know he could not take vengeance on the Roman?
7. How had Leah changed when Daniel returned?

Thought Questions
1. What were Daniel's real motives for going to the festival?
2. What are some other ways of fighting injustice?
3. Why do you think Leah had not been afraid of the Roman?
4. Have you ever done something you later regretted but were unable to undo? What have you found to be the best course of action in that situation?

Chapter 23

Review Questions
1. What was Daniel's hope for Leah?
2. Where had Jesus gone when Daniel arrived in Capernaum?
3. Why did the people call Jesus "Messiah"?
4. What had Jesus offered Simon?
5. How did Simon know God had not forgotten Israel?
6. What did Daniel look for in a leader?
7. What option was left to Daniel?

Thought Questions
1. Why did encounters with Jesus remove guilt? Did they change facts? If not, what did they change?
2. What did Simon mean when he said he already had the kingdom?
3. Does faith always mean "to choose, not knowing"? Why would someone make that choice?

Chapter 24

Review Questions
1. Why couldn't Daniel seek a new band of Zealots?
2. What happened to Leah after the goat died?
3. What did the prospect of Leah's death mean to Daniel?
4. Who came to inquire about Leah? How did Daniel respond?
5. Who arrived at Daniel's house that afternoon?
6. What did Daniel decide when he looked at Jesus? What did he realize?
7. What happened to Leah?

8. What new vow did Daniel and Thacia make?
9. What did Daniel do in response to Jesus' gift?

Thought Questions

1. Is it harder to trust someone after you have been betrayed? Is it possible?
2. Does freedom need a purpose to accompany it? Why or why not?
3. Is vengeance an acceptable way to repay someone? Explain.
4. What did it cost Marcus to approach Daniel? How do you think he felt when Daniel refused him?
5. Why did Daniel feel free to love Thacia?
6. Did Daniel break his vow? Why or why not?

Number the Stars

Lois Lowry

Introduction

Lois Lowry (1937–) spent her childhood traveling the world with her military family. Many of the experiences and relationships she formed during these travels found their way into her books. Lowry has written more than twenty novels, winning the Newbery Medal twice. *Number the Stars* was written in 1989, and won the Newbery in 1990. (Lowry won her second Newbery medal in 1994 for *The Giver.*) In *Number the Stars*, Lowry looks at the events leading up to the Holocaust through the eyes of a young Danish girl.

Reading Practice: Character Chart

In *Number the Stars*, Annemarie lives in a world where much bigger conflicts are beginning to emerge. Her growth is affected by a wide variety of minor characters who come in and out of her family's life. Although many of these characters are not in the book for a long time, they still have an impact on Annemarie. Keeping a character chart while you read this novel will allow you to trace the relationships between the minor and major characters.

As you read, keep a list of the people you encounter, with a few brief notes or arrows indicating relationships between the characters. Jot down comments about the characters' personality traits, appearances, or choices. Include the page number with important points if possible. Pay special attention to the ways Annemarie changes after she encounters each new individual. Keep your character chart nearby, so you can add notes and refer to it as you go.

Going Deeper: Themes

Authors sometimes use minor events, characters, or problems (sub-plots), to reflect or emphasize the main plot. As you read, be on the lookout for characters who share a common fear, flaw, or personality trait. Because the main story of *Number the Stars* is about two girls, Ellen and Annemarie, look for similarities and differences between them. Also think about the relationship between Annemarie and her siblings, and between her family and Ellen's.

Try to identify the main theme of the book, and then look for ways that each character or situation relates to that theme. For example, what does the opening scene of the girls' race have in common with Annemarie's adventure near the end of the book?

Chapter 1

Review Questions

1. Why didn't Ellen want to race Annemarie?
2. What stopped the girls' race?
3. Did Annemarie and Ellen tell their mothers what happened?
4. How did Mrs. Johansen explain the soldiers' unease?
5. What was *De Frie Danske*?
6. Who were the Resistance fighters? How did they operate?
7. What did Kirsti want to eat? Why couldn't she have it?

Thought Questions

1. Why wasn't Kirsti afraid of the soldiers?
2. Why did Mrs. Rosen advise Annemarie to be "one of the crowd"? Do you think of that idea as positive or negative today? How do wars and extreme circumstances change people's priorities?

Chapter 2

Review Questions

1. What kind of story did Kirsti want to hear?
2. Who was the ruler of Denmark? Where did he live?
3. Why did the people love him?
4. Why did thinking about Lise make Annemarie sad?
5. Why didn't the king of Denmark fight the Germans, according to Papa?
6. What was the one country the Germans did not occupy?
7. Even though Annemarie's whole world had changed, what had stayed the same?

Thought Questions

1. Do you think King Christian was a good ruler? Why or why not? What qualifies someone as a good leader during wartimes?
2. Would people today die for their leaders? If not, why not? Should they?
3. Do you think King Christian was right to surrender to the Germans? Explain.
4. Do fairytales ever change? If not, why not? If so, how? Why are familiar things like fairytales so comforting?
5. Can you think of anything that doesn't change? How do you react to change? Is there a right way or a wrong way to think about change? Explain.

Chapter 3

Review Questions

1. Why did Ellen's father dislike the wintertime?
2. What did the girls find at Mrs. Hirsch's button shop?
3. What had Peter brought for Annemarie and Kirsti? For Mama and Papa?
4. What news did Peter bring?
5. How did Mama say the Hirsch family would survive without their shop?
6. Why did Annemarie think she would never be called on for courage?

Thought Questions

1. What does the swastika mean to you? What do you think it means to someone from Germany?
2. Did it harm the Germans to have Jews in business? If not, why did they order the Jewish shops to close?

   3. Annemarie said, "All of Denmark must be bodyguard for the Jews." Explain. Do you agree with her? What does this statement tell you about her character?

   4. Do people die for each other in real life? Is there anyone you would die to protect?

   5. Have you ever been called on for courage? Does courage always require sacrifice?

Chapter 4

Review Questions
1. After what book did Annemarie and Ellen name their paper dolls?
2. Why did Kirsti throw a temper tantrum? How did Ellen get her to stop?
3. What were the Tivoli Gardens?
4. Why was Ellen's New Year different from the Johansens'?
5. Why did Ellen come to stay with the Johansens?
6. Where did Papa propose to hide Ellen?

Thought Questions
1. Why did Kirsti remember the "fireworks"? Was it right for Mama to lie to her?
2. How did Papa respond to the news that King Christian had blown up his own navy? What does that say about King Christian's character? About the qualities Papa admired?
3. When do you think children are old enough to be told about serious things? What determines if someone is old or mature enough to hear a difficult truth?
4. What did "relocation" really mean for the Jews? If the Germans knew what was going to happen, why do you think they used a term meaning "relocate" instead?

Chapter 5

Review Questions
1. What did Ellen want to be when she grew up?
2. How did Lise die?
3. What awakened the girls? What did the soldiers want to know?
4. What did Ellen need to take off? Why?
5. Why didn't the soldier believe Ellen was Annemarie's sister? How did Papa fool the soldiers?

Thought Questions
1. Why didn't Annemarie know how her sister had died? Do you think she was too young to understand?
2. Why did Ellen think it was the worst thing in the world to die young? Do you agree?
3. How did Papa know to get the pictures? Do you think quickly in emergencies? What makes someone calm under pressure? Is it a practiced skill or a gift? Explain.

Chapter 6

Review Questions
1. Where did Papa want to send the girls?
2. Why did Mama say it was safer if she and the girls traveled alone?
3. Why was Papa's telephone conversation strange? What did it mean?
4. What did Kirsti tell the soldiers?

Thought Questions
1. Is education more important than safety? Does the answer change if the decision is for a long-term situation?
2. Why did the soldier ask Mama about the New Year? What was he hoping to find out?
3. Are dreams ever dangerous or harmful? If so, when? How much importance should you attribute to dreams?

Chapter 7

Review Questions
1. What was Uncle Henrik's boat called?
2. What did Mama warn Ellen and Annemarie?
3. Where was Ellen's necklace?
4. About what did Mama tease Uncle Henrik?

Thought Questions
1. What does it mean to look at something with "fresh eyes"? Can you think of an example? In what situations might it be valuable to do that?
2. If the two girls had been in Sweden, looking at Denmark, what might their conversation have been like?

Chapter 8

Review Questions
1. What special treat did the girls have for breakfast?
2. What did the soldiers do with the farmers' butter?
3. What did the code phrase, "weather for fishing," mean?
4. What sad event did Uncle Henrik mention to the girls? Why was Annemarie confused?

Thought Questions
1. Why are ghost stories told at night? What makes the dark frightening?
2. Were Mama and Uncle Henrik lying about Great-aunt Birte? If so, why? Is it okay to lie in that kind of situation?

Chapter 9

Review Questions
1. How did Uncle Henrik answer Annemarie's accusation?
2. Was Great-aunt Birte real?
3. Who came in with Peter?

Thought Questions
1. How brave are you? Does that question make you uncomfortable? Why or why not?
2. Is it possible to be brave and frightened at the same time?
3. Why did Uncle Henrik say it was better not to know everything? Do you agree? Look back at Chapter 4 (Thought Questions). Do you see a theme?

Chapter 10

Review Questions
1. What happened in the middle of the night?
2. What did the soldiers ask Annemarie?
3. How did Mama explain the closed coffin?
4. How did Annemarie describe the world after the officers left?

Thought Questions
1. Can true bonds of friendship be broken? What are the bonds of friendship (the things that create and maintain friendship)?
2. Is it possible for humans to number the stars? Compare this book's use of the phrase to Genesis 15 and Psalm 147. Why do you think Lowry chose this title?
3. How did the Bible verse that Peter read relate to Annemarie and Ellen's situation?

Chapter 11

Review Questions
1. What was inside the coffin?
2. What did Mama give the baby? What did Peter give the baby?
3. What did Peter hand to Mr. Rosen?
4. What caused the commotion at the doorstep?
5. Where was Uncle Henrik taking Ellen and the others?

Thought Questions
1. Why do you think Peter called Mama by her first name? What did it symbolize for him?
2. Annemarie described Peter's comment as, "Only a brief grasp at something that had gone." Explain. What had gone?
3. What is pride? Is there a difference between pride in a job well done and selfish pride? When is it good to be proud?

Chapter 12

Review Questions
1. How long did Annemarie think Mama would be gone?
2. Where did Annemarie find Mama?

Thought Questions
1. Is it harder to do something dangerous or to wait for someone else to do it? Why?
2. What makes waiting difficult?

Chapter 13

Review Questions
1. What had happened to Mama?
2. What did Annemarie find at the foot of the steps?
3. What did Mama ask Annemarie to do?

Thought Questions
1. Was it fair for Mama to ask Annemarie to do something so dangerous? Is protecting children from physical harm a parent's most important responsibility? If not, what is? Think carefully before you answer.

2. Would you have taken the packet without knowing what was in it? Why or why not? What does Annemarie's willingness tell you about her relationship with Mama?

Chapter 14

Review Questions
1. What story did Annemarie think of as she ran through the woods?
2. Why had Uncle Henrik needed to guide the others?
3. What did Annemarie hear? What caused the noise?

Thought Questions
1. Do you, like Kirsti, ask questions when you read? When you watch movies? Why or why not? Do you think people today are expected to absorb messages without thinking about them? If so, why?

Chapter 15

Review Questions
1. How did Annemarie act toward the soldiers?
2. What did the soldiers want to know?
3. Why did the dogs act strangely?
4. What was in the package?
5. Did Annemarie get to the boat on time?

Thought Questions
1. Were you surprised to see what was in the package? How did Lowry build up your expectation that the contents would be different?
2. Why do you think the handkerchief was so important?

Chapter 16

Review Questions
1. Why did Uncle Henrik agree to tell Annemarie about the Rosens?
2. What did Annemarie learn about Peter?
3. Why did the soldiers search the boats?
4. Why was the handkerchief so important?
5. Why did Uncle Henrik say the Rosens would be safe in Sweden?

Thought Questions
1. What does the word "brave" mean to you? Has this book changed your definition?
2. Have you ever become frightened after you did something dangerous? Why?
3. Do all wars end? Explain. Can you think of any counter-examples?

Chapter 17

Review Questions
1. How old was Annemarie when the war ended?
2. What happened to Peter?
3. Why weren't the Johansens able to bury Peter beside Lise?
4. What did Annemarie learn about Lise?
5. Where had Annemarie hidden Ellen's necklace?

Thought Questions
1. If Lise had told her parents what she was doing, do you think they would have let her continue?
2. Do you think young people should get involved in resistance movements? Why or why not? What factors would you take into account to make that decision?
3. Why do you think Annemarie wanted to wear Ellen's necklace?
4. What additional challenges does an author face when writing fiction about tragedies like the Holocaust and World War II? How would you approach the subject?

Amos Fortune, Free Man
Elizabeth Yates

Introduction

Elizabeth Yates (1905–2001) earned recognition for several of her historical novels and biographies of famous individuals. *Amos Fortune, Free Man* was first published in 1950, and won the Newbery Medal in 1951. It is based on the life of an African prince who became a slave in America. In this book, Yates brings Amos Fortune to life, allowing readers to experience his journey to freedom.

Reading Practice: Chronologies

A timeline allows you to visualize the events of a book in chronological order. *Amos Fortune* is a great book on which to practice this skill because it is divided into sections chronologically by year. As you read, create a timeline for Amos's life. Include the major events and turning points, and draw arrows from earlier events to the later events they influence.

Notice that some sections cover a single year, while others span thirty years or more. What does that suggest to you about Yates's vision of Amos's life? What periods of his life did she choose to emphasize? What are some possible reasons? Also keep in mind the challenges a biographer faces if she cannot find enough information about a particular period in her subject's life.

Going Deeper: Genre

Unlike some of the other novels you have encountered, *Amos Fortune, Free Man* was written about an actual man who lived in the 1700s. When you read a biography, you may have to approach it in a slightly different manner. Some of the questions that are a matter of opinion in a fictional book will have correct and incorrect answers in a biography. At the same time, in some ways *Amos Fortune* is historical fiction. To re-create Amos's life, Yates had to choose details to include and omit. She had to create dialogue, and she had to turn historical documents and records into a narrative that would come alive for readers.

As you read, imagine you were writing a biography of someone you know. What incidents would you use to demonstrate their character? How would you structure the book? What sources would you use to gather information? Think about the kind of information Yates might have used to craft her story about Amos, and be on the lookout for places where she might have needed to fill in gaps in the story using her own imagination.

Africa 1725

Review Questions
1. On what occasion does the book open?
2. What was At-mun's role in the tribe?
3. Who was Ath-mun?
4. Who were the invaders?
5. Whom did they kill?
6. Which of the At-mun-shi were left behind? Why?
7. What was At-mun's reminder to his sister as he was taken away?

Thought Questions
1. What is your impression of the At-mun-shi from Yates's description of the culture?
2. What do you associate with the word "pagan"? Does it have a positive or negative connotation? How does Yates seem to use it here?
3. If the At-mun-shi were a freedom-loving people, why didn't they fight back?
4. What work did At-mun believe he was born to do? Do you think leadership is a role someone takes on, or an identity (who they are)? Does it make a difference?

The Middle Passage

Review Questions

1. What significance did At-mun's presence have for the At-mun-shi?
2. Why didn't At-mun attack during the night on the canoe?
3. Where was the *White Falcon* going?
4. Describe the ship's discipline.
5. How long did the Middle Passage take?
6. What was At-mun's "defect"?
7. Who became At-mun's master? What new name did he give At-mun?

Thought Questions
1. Why did At-mun keep his head up? What did it symbolize to him? To his captors?
2. Discuss Yates's portrayal of African spirituality. How does this part of the book prepare you for At-mun's later encounters with Christianity? What does it tell you about his character?
3. Why do you think the pits caused individual differences between the captives to fade? How did the pits transform men and women into animals?
4. Look closely through this chapter in At-mun's life. What specific examples demonstrate the slave traders' failure to think of the slaves as human beings?
5. Why couldn't the master of the *White Falcon* land his cargo on a Sunday? Were the townspeople who made the rule more hypocritical than the slave traders? Explain.
6. Why do you think the auctioneer said none of the slaves had names? Along the same lines, be thinking about the book's title, which uses the name given to At-mun by the auctioneer rather than the name with which he was born.

Boston 1725–1740

Review Questions
1. What was Caleb's trade?
2. Who best understood Amos in the Copeland household?
3. What changed after Amos's and Roxanne's conversation about the Bible verse?
4. What is "manumission"?

5. Why didn't Amos want his freedom yet?
6. Whom did Amos look for at the harbor?
7. What name did Amos plan to take when he was freed?
8. Why was Amos sold? To whom was he sold?

Thought Questions
1. Is it ever kind to withhold freedom? Do you agree with Celia? Did she have the right to make that decision for Amos? Several years later, the Declaration of Independence would call liberty an "inalienable right." Is it being treated that way here?
2. Is it necessary to earn freedom? To learn how to use it? Explain. Is there a difference?
3. Celia said of Amos, "He will not give [his name] up until he can replace it with something of equal meaning." What do Amos's names (At-mun and Amos) symbolize?
4. In what circumstances and for what reasons would freedom be harder than slavery? Yates seems to suggest that Caleb could not have been Amos's protector if Amos were free. Do you agree? Why or why not?

Woburn 1740–1779

Review Questions
1. How did Ichabod Richardson treat his slaves?
2. What request did Amos make of Mr. Richardson?
3. What did Amos give Mrs. Richardson? How did that gift change Amos's purpose in life?
4. When did Amos gain his freedom?
5. Who was Amos's first wife? How long did she live after they were married?
6. Why did Amos fall in love with Lydia?
7. How did Amos wage his war for freedom?

Thought Questions
1. How could slavery affect even something as natural as singing?
2. Do you agree with Amos's comparison of Sundays to white skin?
3. Do Christians today put emphasis on church attendance? Is it important? Why?
4. What sort of picture of slavery does Yates present? Does this book place more emphasis on Amos's personal courage and patience or the horrors of slavery? What would be the pros and cons of each approach to writing about slavery?
5. How did Americans justify owning slaves while they were fighting for liberty from England? Why do you think slaves and former slaves chose to fight in the war?
6. Why was it so important to Amos that Lily die free?
7. Is marriage a strange way to win someone's freedom? Is that intent consistent with the purpose of marriage?

Journey to Keene 1779

Review Questions
1. Who was Amos's third wife?
2. For what kind of sign did Amos ask God?
3. What did Amos take in exchange for his leather in Keene?
4. How long did Amos save to buy Violet and Celyndia?
5. How did Celyndia react to freedom?

Thought Questions
1.   What is the "shadow" side of freedom, according to Amos?
2.   Why didn't Amos complain about the unfair treatment he received from white people? Is it worthwhile to complain, even if nothing changes?
3.   Amos said, "Some things are too wonderful even for a child, and freedom's one of them." Do children experience more or less freedom than adults?
4.   Can a free person appreciate freedom as much as someone who has been enslaved?

The Arrival at Jaffrey

Review Questions
1.   Why did Amos need to have extra money before he could move?
2.   Why was Violet nervous about the move?
3.   Describe the village of Jaffrey.
4.   What did the constable advise Amos and his family to do?
5.   How did Parson Ainsworth greet Amos and his family?
6.   From whom did Amos receive land?

Thought Questions
1.   Was Amos more of a king in Africa or in America? Explain.
2.   Why wasn't the constable free to welcome Amos? Is an elected official always bound to express the will of the people, even if the people are wrong? Discuss.
3.   How do you express thankfulness? What does Amos's response to Parson Ainsworth's generosity tell you about his character?

Hard Work Fills the Iron Kettle 1781–1789

Review Questions
1.   How did Violet and Celyndia help Amos?
2.   Explain the tanning process.
3.   For what was Amos saving his money?
4.   What does "Monadnock" mean?
5.   Why didn't Violet like Lois Burdoo?
6.   What did Violet do with the iron kettle? Why did she do it?

Thought Questions
1.   How does having a dream change a person? Is there a difference between dreams and long-term goals?
2.   Why were black people confined to a separate pew in the church? Why did it take eight years for Amos to receive membership? What do these examples tell you about the way prejudice spreads and lasts in a community?
3.   An elder said, "What a pity [Amos] isn't white. He could do so much for the church." How would you respond if someone made a similar comment about you or someone you knew? Discuss.

Amos on the Mountain

Review Questions
1.   What did Amos decide to do with his money?
2.   How did Amos and Violet decide who was right and who was wrong?
3.   When did Amos become a landowner?

Thought Questions
1. Is there a difference between doing the right thing and doing something for the right reasons? If so, what is it?
2. Which one do you think Violet did when she took Amos's money? What does her choice tell you about her character?
3. Does freedom have to be earned? Look back at "Boston 1725–1740" (Thought Questions). Do you see a theme?

Auctioned for Freedom

Review Questions
1. In what new way did the people of Jaffrey come to trust Amos?
2. What was Celyndia's burden?
3. What is a *Vendue*?
4. Whom did Amos purchase?
5. What happened to Polly? Why was Amos grateful?

Thought Questions
1. Is it right that Amos had to earn his equality? How is equality different from freedom? Is equality a natural right? Should it be?
2. Why do you think the Burdoos were unable to improve themselves? Was it their fault?
3. Amos said, "It does a man no good to be free until he knows how to live, how to walk in step with God." Do you agree? Does this idea justify slavery? Are there different types of freedom?

Evergreen Years 1794–1801

Review Questions
1. Who became Amos's new apprentice? Why?
2. For whose sake had Amos done so many good things?
3. What had happened when Amos had delivered the hide to the Tavern?
4. What did Amos put in his will? What gift did he give the church? The school?
5. When did Amos die?
6. What did Parson Ainsworth write on Amos's tombstone?

Thought Questions
1. Why do you think Amos treasured Charlie's apprenticeship papers? What did they symbolize for him?
2. What did Amos mean when he said he would not "put himself in bondage again" after the incident at the Tavern? Is anger ever the appropriate response to injustice?
3. Do you think people would stop causing suffering if they knew they were doing it? Why or why not?
4. Why did Amos say of the silver communion service, "nothing […] would carry further the whole meaning of his life"?
5. How were Amos's gifts designed to free the white men? Do you think they succeeded?
6. What do you think someone else would write about you on your tombstone?
7. After reading Amos's story, discuss what freedom means to you.

The Door in the Wall
Marguerite de Angeli

Introduction

Marguerite de Angeli (1889–1987) first worked as an illustrator before she began writing books of her own. She researched and wrote children's books about diverse communities in America, including Amish, African-American, Quaker, and Swedish families. *The Door in the Wall*, a story about a lame boy living in the Middle Ages, was published in 1949 and received the Newbery Medal in 1950.

Reading Practice: Glossary of Terms

Because *The Door in the Wall* is set in the Middle Ages, some of the language and terminology will probably be new for you. For example, in the first two paragraphs are the phrases "the hour of Nones" and "his liege lord." Unless you have some familiarity with feudal society, you probably wouldn't know that in the Christian church, "Nones" was the ninth hour of the day (three o'clock in the afternoon), and "liege" meant "entitled to allegiance." Other words are still in use but have changed meanings over time. For example, the word "cell" originally referred to any small room or unit in a larger building. "Cell" did not begin to refer to prisons until the early eighteenth century, because until then, prisoners were not kept in solitary confinement.

Keeping a glossary of unfamiliar terms is a great way to improve your vocabulary and research skills, but more importantly, if you try to figure out new words only by their context, you risk missing important details of the story and setting. So in your reading, if you come across an unfamiliar word, take a minute to write it down along with a brief definition. Keep your glossary beside you for quick reference as you read.

Going Deeper: Symbolism

In literature, sometimes a simple object or action represents something much larger. In this novel, Robin frequently finds meaning in small memories of his father and other mentors. In the first few paragraphs, the weight of his father's glove means more to him than simply the feel of pressure on his arm. As you read, be on the lookout for this and other kinds of symbolism. Pay attention to what Robin remembers and when he remembers it. The phrase in the title, the "door in the wall," appears several times throughout the novel. Think about the ways it is used and the way Robin uses it to find his courage.

Chapter 1

Review Questions

1. Who was Robin's father? What did his father's occupation mean for Robin?
2. What had happened after Robin's mother left?
3. How did Robin compensate for being unable to see out the window?
4. Why did Dame Ellen leave? Why had the other servants fled?
5. Who came to see Robin? Where did the visitor propose to take Robin?
6. How did the visitor encourage Robin to make the journey?

Thought Questions

1. Did the people in Robin's world have freedom to choose their own path in life? How is that different today? Do your parents' jobs or accomplishments place certain expectations on you? Can you choose not to accept these obligations?
2. How would you respond to a handicap like Robin's? What does Robin's innovative way of "seeing" out the window tell you about his character?
3. Do you have weaknesses for which you have had to compensate? What did you learn from the experience?
4. Brother Luke said, "Thou hast only to follow the wall far enough and there will be a door in it." Explain. Do you agree?

Chapter 2

Review Questions

1. Describe Brother Luke's cell.
2. What activity did Robin begin under Brother Luke's tutelage?
3. What items did he make?
4. What happened in the corridor after Robin and Brother Luke left the scriptorium?
5. How were people named in Robin's time?

Thought Questions

1. Do herbs have real health benefits? How would you distinguish between superstition and legitimate medicinal uses in Brother Luke's description of herb lore?
2. What does the practice of naming people after their occupation, physical features, or character traits tell you about Robin's society? Why aren't people named this way now?
3. Where does your name come from? What do popular methods of selecting names today tell you about your society?

Chapter 3

Review Questions

1. Where did Brother Luke take Robin? Who showed him how to finish the cross?
2. Why did Robin become angry? How did Brother Matthew rebuke him?
3. What, according to Brother Luke, are the keys to healing?
4. What did Brother Luke say about Robin's letter to his father?

Thought Questions

1. Do you blame other people when you are angry? Why do you think people need someone to blame when something goes wrong?
2. Do you agree with Brother Luke that God's good time, sunshine, love, and a bright

spirit lead to healing? What would today's doctors and scientists say? Discuss.

3. In what way are reading and writing "doors in the wall"?

Chapter 4

Review Questions
1. What was Robin's next carving project that summer?
2. What happened when Robin went fishing at the brook with Brother Luke?
3. What was Robin's secret that showed he was well?
4. Where did Brother Luke take Robin to get the padding and leather for his crutches?

Thought Questions
1. Is it inspiring or discouraging for you to see others doing things you cannot do? Why?
2. Brother Luke said, "Crutches or crosses as thou'lt have it. 'Tis all the same thing." A crutch supports you, while a cross afflicts you. "Crosses" also refers to the crosspieces at the top of the crutch. Why do you think de Angeli chose to make Brother Luke's words ambiguous? What does the similarity between the two words symbolize?

Chapter 5

Review Questions
1. What message came to Robin from his father?
2. Who were Robin's traveling companions?
3. Why did the travelers get lost? Where did they spend the night?

Thought Questions
1. What is a *pilgrimage*? Was Robin's journey a pilgrimage? What did Brother Luke say? Do you agree?
2. Why did Brother Luke, a devout friar, refer to the outdoors as Mother Nature? Do you think the name had a different meaning for him?

Chapter 6

Review Questions
1. Did the host at the sign of the Shepherd's Bush hope for peace? Why or why not?
2. Why did Brother Luke mistrust the White Hart Inn?
3. What happened that night? How did the travelers escape?

Thought Questions
1. Was Brother Luke talking about literal or figurative wrong turns? Have you ever taken a wrong turn in life? How far away from the right road did you get before you stopped?
2. How would the adventure have ended if Robin had said at any point, "I'm lame; I can't do it"? Why didn't he? What does that tell you about his character?

Chapter 7

Review Questions
1. What was happening at Wychwood Bec when the travelers arrived? Describe the event.
2. Where did the travelers spend the night?
3. Who welcomed Robin to Lindsay?
4. Who or what were the primary threats to Lindsay? What was the castle's weakness?
5. What animal became Robin's friend?

Thought Questions
1. Where do you think the idea for grand churches originated? Can man-made structures have the same splendor as that found in nature? Discuss.
2. Is everyone capable of some service? Can you think of any exceptions? What determines an individual's worth?

Chapter 8

Review Questions
1. What was Robin learning to make under John-go-in-the-Wynd's tutoring?
2. For what three reasons did Brother Luke recommend swimming in cold water?
3. How did Robin win the approval of Alan-at-Gate?
4. Why was the fog dangerous? What happened as a result of the fog?

Thought Questions
1. Explain: "It is better to have crooked legs than a crooked spirit." Do you agree?
2. What was Brother Luke's measure of success? How is that different from popular measures of success today? Which one shows greater wisdom? Discuss.
3. When the castle was attacked, what instructions did Sir Peter give? What do they tell you about the values of English society? About Sir Peter's character?

Chapter 9

Review Questions
1. Describe the siege of the castle. What was the final straw for the besieged people?
2. Who was the only possible source of help? What did Robin propose to do?
3. Who stopped Robin on the way? How did Robin escape?
4. What was the signal for the attack?
5. Why were Sir Peter and Sir Hugh on bad terms?
6. How did John and Robin get into the town?

Thought Questions
1. How was warfare different in Robin's time than it is today? How was it the same?
2. What do you think was the hardest part of Robin's task? Why?
3. What skills had Brother Luke and John taught Robin that prepared him for this task? Include physical as well as emotional preparation in your analysis.

Chapter 10

Review Questions
1. Was the counterattack a success?
2. How were John and Robin rewarded?
3. Who arrived on Christmas Eve? How did they react to the crutches?
4. What did the King give Robin?
5. Where did Robin plan to go after Christmas?

Thought Questions
1. How did Robin change by the end of the book? Why did the changes make him fearful to see his parents again?
2. Robin's father told Robin he "[could not] see whether or no your legs are misshapen." Was he ignoring Robin's misfortune, or is there another explanation?
3. Is it symbolic that Robin's family was reunited on Christmas Eve? Discuss.
4. What was Robin's "door in the wall"?

The Secret Garden
Frances Hodgson Burnett

Introduction

Frances Hodgson Burnett (1849–1924) was born in England but moved to the United States as a teenager, where she began writing as a means of supporting her younger siblings. During her lifetime, she wrote a number of children's and adult novels, as well as several successful plays. *The Secret Garden* was written in 1909. It is set in England and explores the changing lives of three children who help each other grow in their appreciation for life and its beauty.

Reading Practice: Maps

Look up examples of architectural blueprints, house plans, or floor plans. Pay attention to the way the designers depict doors, windows, hallways, furniture, and multiple stories or levels.

From information in the text, draw a map of the house and grounds of Misselthwaite Manor, and include as many of the rooms and gardens as you can, with their approximate locations. Use your imagination where details are lacking. Take note of descriptive adjectives like "gloomy," "crowded," and "airy," and try to reflect those characteristics in your imagined architecture.

Going Deeper: Worldview

In *The Secret Garden*, Mary spends part of her childhood in India before she is transplanted to England. One of the reasons she finds the transition hard is that she has been raised with a set of assumptions about the way the world works. As you read, think about what her expectations are and how they change as she interacts with Martha, Dickon, and Colin.

Several other worldviews are represented in this book as well. Mrs. Sowerby's family demonstrates a commitment to healthy families, hard work, thoughtful education, and care for the natural world. When their joy of living begins to rub off on Mary and Colin, the children recognize that something is changing. As Colin says, "I don't know its name, so I call it Magic." Although the word "magic" has many associations, ask yourself how the children are using it here. What is the source of the things they call magic? Is there another word that could replace "Magic" without changing the meaning?

For parents, this is a great opportunity to respond with wisdom as you discuss these questions with your children. For students, this is a great exercise in thinking critically about the power of words and the underlying assumptions of the books you read.

Chapter 1

Review Questions
1. Who was Mary Lennox? Why was she so bad-tempered?
2. What was an *Ayah*?
3. Why did Mary stare at her mother?
4. Why was it so quiet when Mary awoke?

Thought Questions
1. Does being wanted affect a child's disposition? How much should your family shape who you are? Explain.
2. What is your impression of India from Burnett's description? Is it positive or negative? Pay attention to the adjectives Burnett uses to describe the Indian people and Mary's family. How does this chapter create a foundation for Mary's personality?
3. How did Mary expect to be treated? How does she respond to tragedy? Where do you think she learned to behave that way?

Chapter 2

Review Questions
1. How did Mary react to her parents' deaths?
2. How did Mary earn the nickname "Mistress Mary Quite Contrary"?
3. Where was Mary going to be sent?
4. Define *marred*.
5. How did Mrs. Medlock describe Misselthwaite?

Thought Questions
1. How would you have turned out if you had grown up in Mary's situation? Was she to blame for being bad-tempered?
2. Why was Mary surprised to learn that Mr. Craven had been married? What does this reveal about her character?
3. Mary only began to feel sorry for Mr. Craven when she related his life to a fairy tale. Do you use stories to help you understand other people? What is the risk of doing that?

Chapter 3

Review Questions
1. How did Mrs. Medlock's speech change when they got off the train?
2. Describe the moor.
3. Who met Mary and Mrs. Medlock when they arrived at Misselthwaite?

Thought Questions
1. Why do you think Mr. Craven did not want to see Mary?
2. In your opinion, why did he bring her to England? Is obligation a good reason to

do something? Can bad motives spoil a good action?

Chapter 4

Review Questions
1. What awakened Mary in the morning?
2. How was Martha different from the servants to whom Mary was accustomed?
3. What did Martha think Mary would look like?
4. How had Martha's family life been different from Mary's?
5. Why was one of the gardens locked up?
6. Whom did Mary meet in the gardens? What did he tell her about herself?
7. Why did the robin come? Where did he live?

Thought Questions
1. What words did Burnett use to describe Martha? How do these words create a contrast between Mary and Martha?
2. What was Martha's impression of India? How did the two girls view people of other races? Were Martha's prejudices different than Mary's?
3. How are customs and traditions built? Who enforces them? What customs, if any, do you follow? Why do you follow them?
4. Does ignorance make you indifferent to the suffering of others?
5. Has anyone ever told you something unpleasant but true about yourself? How did you react? Is it always best to be bluntly honest?

Chapter 5

Review Questions
1. Why was it good for Mary to go outside? How did she begin to change?
2. Where did she go most often? Whom did she see there?
3. Why did Mr. Craven hate the garden?
4. What is *wutherin'*?
5. What four good things had happened to Mary since she had come to Misselthwaite?
6. What did Mary hear? How did Martha explain the noise?

Thought Questions
1. Whom do you think Mr. Craven blamed for his wife's death? Explain your answer.
2. What do you think was behind the changes taking place in Mary? What did she need that life on the moor was able to provide?

Chapter 6

Review Questions
1. What did Martha suggest Mary do to amuse herself while it was raining?
2. What did Mary decide to do instead? Why didn't she ask permission?
3. What did Mary hear while she was lost?
4. Who appeared from behind the tapestry?

Thought Questions
1. Why do you think closed doors and locked places are so fascinating?
2. How did you learn to ask permission?
3. Describe one of the rooms Mary entered. What impression of Mr. and Mrs. Craven

do you get from the description of the house?

4. How can you tell when someone is lying? Did the lies Martha and Mrs. Medlock told Mary seem consistent with their characters? If not, why would they lie to her?

Chapter 7

Review Questions

1. Describe the moor after the storm.
2. Where did Mary want to go?
3. What did Ben tell Mary about the locked garden?
4. What did the robin show Mary?

Thought Questions

1. Do you think Mary was correct in saying no one liked her? Is it always important to be liked? To like yourself? Think carefully before you answer.
2. Describe the relationship in this book between people and nature. How do the people interact with nature? How do they speak of it? Do they value it? In what way?

Chapter 8

Review Questions

1. What did Mary intend to do with the key?
2. What did Martha's mother say when Martha told her about Mary?
3. What did Martha bring back for Mary?
4. What did Mary find when the wind blew?

Thought Questions

1. Was it stealing for Mary to keep the key? Why or why not?
2. What did Mary emphasize in her stories about India? What did she leave out?
3. Does it seem strange for Martha's family to pity Mary? Explain.
4. What do you think Mary meant by "magic"? How did she hear about it? How would you explain the things she called magic?

Chapter 9

Review Questions

1. What made the secret garden so different from other gardens?
2. What did Mary do to improve the garden?
3. What did Mary want to buy? How did she get the things?
4. What had Martha asked her mother on Mary's behalf?
5. How did Martha explain the crying noise?

Thought Questions

1. Is gardening a natural skill or do you have to learn it? What does this book suggest?
2. Why do you think Mary wanted to meet Martha's mother and Dickon? What made them different from Mary's family?

Chapter 10

Review Questions
1. What improvements did Mary make to the garden? How did the garden change her?
2. What did the robin do to win Ben's approval?
3. What had happened to the roses that belonged to the young lady?
4. What did Dickon look like? How did Mary meet him?
5. How did Dickon know Mary was friends with the robin?

Thought Questions
1. Is the robin a character in this book? If so, what is his role in the story?
2. How would you describe Ben Weatherstaff? What does he reveal about Mary? What effect does he have on her?
3. Why did Mary compare Dickon to a snake charmer? What allows someone to tame an animal? Does it take a similar skill to relate to other people?
4. Why do you think Mary told Dickon about the secret garden?

Chapter 11

Review Questions
1. Had Dickon known about the secret garden?
2. Were all the roses dead? How did Dickon know?
3. Why did Dickon think someone else had been in the garden?
4. How many people did Mary like?
5. What question did Mary ask Dickon in Yorkshire?
6. Why did Dickon compare Mary to a missel thrush?

Thought Questions
1. What makes people contrary? Is it a decision? An unfulfilled need? How does someone stop being contrary (or angry, or resentful, or cruel)? Do you have to replace those traits with a positive trait like love or compassion or kindness?
2. How many people do you like? Have you ever thought to count? Why or why not? How did Mary's counting reflect the changes taking place in her life?
3. Why do you think Mary compared Dickon to an Indian native? Did she see it as complimentary or insulting? Compare her thoughts here to her conversation with Martha in Chapter 4.

Chapter 12

Review Questions
1. How did Mary describe Dickon to Martha?
2. Who wanted to see Mary after she had her dinner? Why?
3. What did Mary ask for? How did Mr. Craven respond?
4. What had Dickon left for Mary in the garden?

Thought Questions
1. Do you think Mary was being deceptive when she asked for "a bit of earth"? Explain.
2. How do you think Mr. Craven felt about Mary? What makes you think so? Was he a good guardian? What criteria would you use to answer that question?

Chapter 13

Review Questions

1. What symbol did Dickon leave on his note for Mary? How did she interpret it?
2. Why couldn't Mary go back to the garden the next day? What did she do instead?
3. What did Mary find behind the tapestry door?
4. Why didn't Mr. Craven want to see Colin?
5. How did Mary convince Colin that he should not demand to see the garden?
6. What did Colin show Mary behind the curtain?

Thought Questions

1. Why did Colin think he would not live to grow up? Did he really believe that, or was he trying to convince himself? What does this first encounter suggest about his character?
2. When Colin said he didn't want to live or die, what do you think he really wanted?
3. Colin said his father almost hated him because his mother died, and Mary replied that Mr. Craven hated the garden for the same reason. Do you see other similarities between the garden and Colin? Keep this question in mind as you continue to read.
4. Did Colin really hate his mother? Explain. Is hate a convenient emotion when you don't know what you feel? Can you think of other examples in which this might be true?

Chapter 14

Review Questions

1. How did Martha react when Mary told her about finding Colin?
2. What was wrong with Colin, according to Martha?
3. What scene from India did Mary think of when she looked at Colin?
4. What was the "best thing [Mary] could have said" to Colin?
5. Who came into Colin's rooms while Mary was there?

Thought Questions

1. Why do you think Colin let Mary look at him? What made her different?
2. Several times Mary compared people to individuals she saw in India (see Chapter 11). Why do you think she used her childhood in India as a way to understand life in England? Why might that be a problem?
3. When she told Colin about Dickon, Mary said Dickon didn't call his skill with animals "magic." Why do you think Mary and Colin wanted to think of it as magical?
4. Did Dr. Craven give Colin good advice? Why or why not? Why might it be a bad thing to remember that you are ill?

Chapter 15

Review Questions

1. Why didn't Colin like strangers to see him?
2. What creatures did Dickon bring with him to the garden?
3. What was the robin doing in the garden?
4. Had Dickon known about Colin?
5. Did Dickon tell his mother about the garden?
6. What did Dickon say would be good for Colin?

Thought Questions
1. Mary said Colin "knows a good many things out of books but he doesn't know anything else." Could the same statement apply to Mary?
2. What are some similarities and differences between Mary and Colin? Did Colin's weakness make Mary stronger?
3. Do you agree with Mrs. Sowerby that unwanted children almost never thrive? Why?
4. How much power does fear have in your life? What is stronger than fear?

Chapter 16

Review Questions
1. What did Mary do to offend Colin?
2. What made Mary angry with Colin? Was she being hypocritical?
3. Why did the nurse laugh?
4. What did Mr. Craven send Mary?
5. What ailed Colin, according to the nurse? From what did his tantrums stem?

Thought Questions
1. Is it strange to you that Mary was excited about getting fatter? What do you associate with the word "fat"? How are your standards of beauty different than Mary's?
2. Look back at Chapter 13 (Thought Questions). What does the scene in Colin's room suggest about the similarity between Mary and Colin?
3. When is anger a healthy emotion? What makes it an unhealthy one?

Chapter 17

Review Questions
1. What awakened Mary in the middle of the night?
2. What did the nurse ask Mary to do?
3. Did Colin have a lump on his back?
4. What did Colin agree to do with Mary and Dickon?

Thought Questions

1. How might Colin have grown up differently if he had been around other children?
2. Does this book imply that most illness has a mental, not a physical cause? How might you respond differently to someone with a real physical illness?
3. Is the truth always enough to convince people to put aside their superstitions?

Chapter 18

Review Questions
1. According to Mrs. Sowerby, what were the two worst things for a child?
2. What did Dickon say was good for sick people?
3. How did Mary make Colin laugh?
4. What did Mary decide to tell Colin?

Thought Questions
1. Do you think it is better for a child to be neglected or spoiled? Why? Are these two things similar in any way? What type of damage does each one cause?

2. What did Mary, Colin, and Ben Weatherstaff have in common? How did they help each other grow?
3. Why do you think Dickon seemed like an angel to Mary? What does this comparison tell you about her understanding of angels?

Chapter 19

Review Questions

1. Why did Dr. Craven come? What did he expect to find? What did he find?
2. What, according to Mrs. Sowerby, do children learn from other children?
3. How would Dr. Craven have explained Colin's better health in the morning? How did Colin explain it?
4. What did Dickon bring with him when he came to visit?

Thought Questions

1. Why did Mrs. Medlock say Mrs. Sowerby's broad Yorkshire kept her from being clever? Is that a logical argument? Why or why not?
2. Why do you think the animals made it easier for the children to converse?

Chapter 20

Review Questions

1. How did the children arrange to get Colin into the secret garden without being seen?
2. What orders did Colin give Mr. Roach?
3. What did Colin announce when he saw the secret garden?

Thought Questions

1. Was there any magic in Dickon's ability to make Colin and Mary feel better? If not, how did he do it? What unspoken lessons did he teach them?
2. Why do you think the springtime and the garden had such a profound impact on Colin?

Chapter 21

Review Questions

1. How was Colin distracted from the old tree? Why did he need to be distracted?
2. When did Dickon say Colin would walk again?
3. Who interrupted the stillness of the afternoon? Why was he angry?
4. What did the newcomer assume about Colin? How did Colin prove him wrong?

Thought Questions

1. Discuss Dickon's suggestion that Mrs. Craven was looking after Colin. Why do you think people want to believe that their loved ones are still present after they die? Does that belief have any basis in truth?
2. Why do you think Ben was so protective of the garden? What did the garden symbolize for him?

Chapter 22

Review Questions

1. What was the magic, according to Dickon?
2. How had Ben entered the garden? For what purpose?

3. What did Colin want to do before the sun set?

Thought Questions
1. Do you agree with Dickon's definition of magic? What "magic" makes crocuses grow?
2. How did Ben justify breaking orders and coming into the garden? Were his reasons valid? What does his reasoning tell you about his character?
3. Why do you think Burnett used the word "magic" so frequently? Think about Mary's childhood and her love of fantasy books. Think also about the way the children's growth was related to discovering joy in life and seeing ordinary things in a new way.

Chapter 23

Review Questions
1. What was Colin's chief peculiarity, according to Mary?
2. What was Colin's scientific experiment?
3. How did Colin distinguish between the right magic and the wrong magic?
4. Why did Colin want to keep his experiment a secret?

Thought Questions
1. Why was it helpful for the children to think of what happened in the garden as magic?
2. How would you define what Colin called "magic"?
3. Can you make nice things happen by saying they are going to happen? Why or why not?
4. This book was written in 1909, when scientists like Einstein and Pavlov were experimenting with physics and psychology. How do you think this growing interest in science might have influenced Burnett's writing?

Chapter 24

Review Questions
1. Whom did Dickon tell about the secret garden?
2. Why did Colin have to complain from time to time?
3. What made it difficult for Colin to pretend to be ill?
4. How did Mrs. Sowerby help Mary and Colin keep their secret?
5. Where did Dickon learn about exercising?

Thought Questions
1. Was it fair for Colin and Mary to deceive the staff? Was it unkind?
2. Do you think Mary would have changed as much as she did if she had not met Colin? Who do you think is the main focus of the story, Mary or Colin? Why?

Chapter 25

Review Questions
1. Why did the children avoid the robin's corner of the garden?
2. Why did the robin and his mate worry about Colin?
3. What did Mary and Colin do on rainy days?
4. What change did Mary notice in Colin's room?

Thought Questions
1. Why did Colin begin to leave the curtain open over his mother's picture? What does that tell you about his character development?
2. Was Colin's father fond of him, in your opinion? What does it mean to be fond of someone? Are fondness and love the same thing? Explain.
3. Mr. Craven is not physically present in the book very often. Do you think he is an important character? If so, in what way? How does he influence Colin?

Chapter 26

Review Questions
1. Why did Colin practice giving lectures?
2. How did Colin know he was well?
3. Who came into the garden after Dickon sang?
4. What was Mrs. Sowerby's name for magic?

Thought Questions
1. Is there a definite moment when someone becomes well, or is it a gradual process?
2. After Dickon sang the Doxology, Colin said, "Perhaps it means just what I mean when I want to shout out that I am thankful to the Magic." Does his comment change the way you think about the magic in this book?
3. Do you think Colin's "Magic" was another way of recognizing God's work? Explain. How are they different?
4. How do you think Colin and Mary helped Ben Weatherstaff? Why did he suddenly see value in the Doxology?
5. Do you agree with Mrs. Sowerby that names (Magic, The Big Good Thing, God) do not matter? What is the danger in that argument?

Chapter 27

Review Questions
1. What made Mr. Craven feel suddenly alive while he was in Austria?
2. What did Mr. Craven dream?
3. Who wrote to Mr. Craven? What did she ask him to do?
4. How did Colin meet his father? What was Mr. Craven's reaction when he saw his son?

Thought Questions
1. "To let a sad thought or a bad one get into your mind is as dangerous as letting a scarlet fever germ get into your body. If you let it stay there after it has got in, you may never get over it as long as you live." Explain. Do you agree?
2. Can two opposite things exist in the same person or place (happiness and sadness, for example)?
3. Was Mr. Craven a bad father? What makes someone a good father? If the book continued, do you think Mr. Craven and Colin's relationship would be better?

Carry On, Mr. Bowditch
Jean Lee Latham

Introduction

Jean Lee Latham (1902–1995) had a gift for bringing the historical to life. Her biographies of famous Americans, including Eli Whitney and Sam Houston, have been widely acclaimed. *Carry On, Mr. Bowditch* was published in 1955, and won the Newbery Medal in 1956. This novel traces the life of Nathaniel Bowditch, a talented navigator, astronomer, and mathematician from the late eighteenth century, and gives a true example of what it means to love learning.

Reading Practice: Glossary of Terms

Nathaniel Bowditch is a great example of someone who took responsibility for his own education. Each time he had to learn a new subject, whether Latin, French, navigation, or mathematics, he started by keeping a notebook of the basic facts, the grammar, of the subject. As you read about his adventures, you'll be introduced to some of the vocabulary he needed to know to sail, navigate, and perform calculations, and some of the terms will probably be new for you.

This is your chance to employ one of Mr. Bowditch's learning tools as you read about his life. In your reading, if you come across an unfamiliar word or term, take a minute to look it up and write it down along with a brief definition. Keep your glossary beside you for quick reference as you read. It may be helpful to separate your glossary into general vocabulary and vocabulary that is specialized to a particular field (navigation or chandlery, for example).

Going Deeper: Themes

Authors sometimes use minor events, characters, or problems (sub-plots), to reflect or emphasize the main plot. Even though *Carry On, Mr. Bowditch* is historical fiction, it is still fiction. It is impossible to include every detail about an individual's life in a few hundred pages, so Latham had to choose which events to include and which to leave out or mention only briefly. As a result, the story you read is structured around key ideas or themes in Nat's life.

As you read, ask yourself what the situations that confront Nat have in common. Think about the way he handles difficult situations and how he approaches challenging tasks. Be on the lookout for repeated phrases used by Nat or by people he encounters. Try to identify the main theme of the book, and then look for ways that each character or situation relates to that theme.

Chapter 1

Review Questions

1. Why did Nat want to stay awake?
2. What bad luck had come to Nat's family?
3. Why didn't Nat complete his good-luck spell?
4. What did Granny ask Nat to fetch from the neighbors?
5. What prevented Nat from performing his good-luck spell in Salem?

Thought Questions

1. If luck is random chance, why did Nat think he could influence it? Is there such a thing as luck? Why do you think people want to believe in good or bad luck? Discuss.
2. Would you go to your neighbors if you needed to borrow something? If not, why not? What does your answer suggest about society's "rules" for proper behavior?
3. Are there certain jobs that are "men's work" and "women's work"? Do you think it is the job of boys to look after girls and women? How have ideas about these questions changed since Nat's time? Discuss.

Chapter 2

Review Questions

4. What is a *privateer*?
5. Why did Granny tell Father to take Nat with him to the wharves?
6. What did Father say he would do if he had money?
7. What is an *expectation*? How did the sailor respond to Nat's offer to buy one?
8. Why did the sailor tell Nat not to mention their bargain?

Thought Questions

1. Do you think privateers and pirates are the same? If not, how are they different?
2. Are ethics different during wartime? Should they be? Give arguments for each side.
3. Why did Father call himself a Jonah? Look back at the biblical story. Was Jonah's problem bad luck? If not, why did he bring danger on the sailors?
4. Why did Father ask Nat if it was better to go back to his trade? Do you think he knew the answer? Do you think he expected Nat to know?

Chapter 3

Review Questions

1. What question did Nat answer in school? Why was he counted wrong?
2. Why did Nat prefer arithmetic to history?
3. What did Father ask Master Watson to do for Nat?
4. Why did Master Watson accuse Nat of lying? How did he test Nat's truthfulness?
5. What news did Nat hear about the *Pilgrim*? What had happened to Tom Perry?
6. What did a fisherman's people do when a fisherman died at sea?

Thought Questions
1. What was Master Watson's reaction when he heard Nat had been to school for two years in Danvers? What does his response tell you about his views of women?
2. What makes math a precise subject? Are any other subjects equally precise? Does that mean math is the best or most important subject? Why or why not?
3. What makes books so valuable? Were they more valuable in Nat's time? If so, why?
4. Why did people say those like Tom "died heroes"? What is a *hero*? Do you have to die to become one? Is it comforting to know someone died a hero? Discuss.

Chapter 4

Review Questions
1. What kind of ship was the *Freedom*? Why did Hab show her to Nat?
2. Why had Hab lied about being cold the previous winter?
3. Why did the ship owners think the war was almost over?
4. What caused the commotion in the middle of the night? Who was John Derby?
5. When was the peace announced?
6. What was "crowding sail"? Why was it dangerous?
7. What does it mean to "lose your anchor to windward"?
8. Why did Nat have to leave school? How did Mother comfort him?

Thought Questions
1. Why did Hab think boys shouldn't blubber? What does this statement tell you about his character? What does Nat's response tell you about his relationship with Hab?
2. How does inflation work? What are products really worth? Why is paper money less stable than precious metals?
3. Are peace and the absence of war the same thing? Why or why not?
4. Mother said "If you look at the stars long enough, it helps. It shrinks your day-to-day troubles down to size." What does looking at the stars actually change?

Chapter 5

Review Questions
1. Whom did Nat crash into on the street? What did the man tell Mother?
2. What happened to Mother right before Christmas?
3. What happened to Granny two years later?
4. What did Nat overhear during the night? How did he interpret it?
5. Who were Ropes and Hodges? What were the terms of the indenture?

Thought Questions
1. Why did Nat and Mary say Father had "lost his last anchor to windward"?
2. Have you ever misinterpreted something you heard? Why is it dangerous to listen in on conversations that are not meant for you?
3. Nat listened to his father's conversation because he wanted to know the truth. Why, then, do you think he kept his family from knowing the truth about his feelings? Are the two examples of withholding information the same? Why or why not?

Chapter 6

Review Questions

1. Why wasn't Nat happy about Mr. Walsh's praise?
2. How did Lizza describe being indentured? What were the conditions of Nat's indenture?
3. What sailing term did Ben Meeker use to describe Nat?
4. What did Sam Smith say it meant to "sail by ash breeze"?
5. Why did Mr. Hodges give Nat a notebook?
6. How did the log work? How was the log different from "keeping a log"?

Thought Questions

1. Does indenturing sound like a fair bargain? Why or why not? Why do you think people no longer use this practice?
2. What was the primary difference between Ben Meeker's and Sam Smith's perspectives on difficult situations? Which one is the most similar to your own?
3. Have you ever "sailed by ash breeze"? Explain. What does Nat's response to Sam's description tell you about his character?
4. What are some practical uses for math? Do you think about the fact that you are using math in everyday life?

Chapter 7

Review Questions

1. What did Nat do in the evenings after he finished work?
2. What did Mr. Ropes ask Nat to look up? How did Nat misunderstand him?
3. What does an almanac tell you?
4. What did the stranger offer Nat after he saw Nat's almanac?

Thought Questions

1. Why do you think Nat put so much effort into his notebooks?
2. Describe Nat's method of learning about subjects. How do you learn best? How much time do you put into voluntary learning?
3. Do you think you would have the willpower to "sail by ash breeze" for nine years?

Chapter 8

Review Questions

1. What caused the excitement in town on the day of Hab's visit?
2. Which book on astronomy did Dr. Bentley give Nat? Why couldn't he read it?
3. What tools did Dr. Bentley give Nat to assist him in learning Latin?
4. What did Nat overhear about the chandlery on one of his trips to town?
5. What did Mr. Ward tell Nat? What did the news mean for Nat's dreams?

Thought Questions

1. What books did you use the first time you learned a language? Do you think you could learn a language using Nat's method?
2. How do you respond to disappointment? Compare your way to Nat's. How is his response consistent with what you have already seen of his character?

Chapter 9

Review Questions

1. What had Mr. Hodges suggested to Mr. Ward?
2. What kind of math did Nat use to compliment Lizza?
3. Why didn't Mary want to marry David Martin? How did Nat convince her?
4. What did Dr. Prince offer Nat?
5. What happened to Lizza?
6. What did Elizabeth give Nat? Why?

Thought Questions

1. Does being happy take practice? How would you practice it?
2. What did Lizza mean when she said Elizabeth had "eyes in the back of her heart"?
3. Why, according to Elizabeth, did Nat read Latin? Does a restless mind come naturally, or do you have to cultivate it?
4. How does a good mind help you deal with hardships? When might the ability to think not be sufficient? On what do you rely when your brain fails you?

Chapter 10

Review Questions

1. Who was Nathan Read? To what new field of study did he introduce Nat?
2. Why did Mr. Jordy say Nat needed to learn proper French pronunciation?
3. Explain Elizabeth's analogy of the chair and Nat's brain.
4. What happened to Captain Boardman?
5. How can you tell time by the stars?
6. What gift did Mr. Hodges give Nat in the note?

Thought Questions

1. Is pronunciation always important when you study a language? Defend your answer.
2. Do you think English pronunciation makes sense? Why or why not?
3. What is *intuition*? Did Elizabeth really know when her father's ship would arrive?
4. Why do you think the freedom following indenture caused such a shock for some people? Was it similar to the freedom Amos Fortune (from *Amos Fortune, Free Man*) experienced when he became a free man? Why or why not? What is the difference between an indentured servant and a slave?
5. In different parts of America, slaves and indentured servants existed at the same time. Do you think the system of slavery and the indenture system are related in any way? What is the biggest difference in the mindset behind those systems?

Chapter 11

Review Questions

1. Why were American ships being attacked?
2. Why was Nat indignant about the editorial?
3. Did Dr. Bentley agree with Ben? Explain his view of censorship.
4. Why did Captain Gibaut say America needed a navy? What job did he offer Nat?
5. What was a *venture*? What did Nat choose for his venture?
6. Why did Captain Gibaut decide not to command the *Henry*?

Thought Questions
1. Dr. Bentley said, "We can't have freedom—unless we have freedom." Explain. Do you agree? Do people still need to hear that statement today? In what situations?
2. Can censorship ever be justified? If so, when? Think carefully about the proper role of government before you answer.
3. Compare ventures to the stock market. Does one involve a greater risk? When is that type of risk justifiable?

Chapter 12

Review Questions
1. What two things did Mr. Derby forbid the ship to do?
2. In what way were surveying and navigation different?
3. What did Nat propose to use to find their longitude? Why was Captain Prince skeptical?
4. How did the men respond to Nat's teaching? Why did Nat teach them?
5. How did Nat explain his accuracy with the lunar?

Thought Questions
1. Do you think Nat's experience as an indentured servant had anything to do with his opposition to the slave trade?
2. Can book learning substitute for practical experience? Give reasons for both answers.
3. Can everyone learn? Think carefully before you answer.
4. Do you think knowledge would make sailors more or less likely to rebel? Explain.
5. Who started the business of rebelling against unjust rulers? Go back as far into history as you can to answer. Are revolutions contagious?

Chapter 13

Review Questions
1. Why had Bourbon changed because of the Revolution? What was its new name?
2. What had happened to the harbor? How did this change the *Henry's* plans?
3. How had the Frenchmen tricked Captain Blanchard?
4. What did Nat find while studying Moore's *Navigator*?
5. What was Nat's new way of working lunars?
6. What did Dr. Bentley tell Nat when he returned to Salem?

Thought Questions
1. Why did the leaders of the French Revolution insist on calling everyone "Citizen"?
2. Why did Captain Blanchard's tactic of impressing the Frenchmen fail? Why did they want to take advantage of him?
3. Is anyone above making mistakes? Have you ever assumed someone was? What happened? How important is one small mistake? Was Nat overreacting? Why or why not?

Chapter 14

Review Questions
1. What did Mary want to tell Nat?
2. Where did Mr. Derby want to send Nat and Captain Prince next? What language did Nat need to learn for the voyage?

3. Why was Mr. Collins upset with Nat for teaching the sailors?
4. What did Elizabeth do right before Nat left?
5. What did Mr. Pintard tell Nat about the legend of Machico?

Thought Questions
1. Latham describes the deaths of Nat's friends and families in very brief, straightforward sentences. What is the effect of this technique? How does it fit into Nat's way of dealing with hardships?
2. Some of the men Nat taught were able to take new, better positions as a result. If you have the ability to do so, is moving up in a career always the best choice? Discuss.
3. Do you think Lem Harvey's training methods were effective? Why or why not?

Chapter 15

Review Questions
1. What was Lem Harvey's problem?
2. What did Nat offer the crew? What was their response?
3. What kind of ship approached the *Astrea*? Whose colors was she flying?
4. What, according to Nat, prevented Lem from learning?
5. What made the men think the sea was on fire?
6. Why did the other ship pass the *Astrea* in Sundra Strait?

Thought Questions
1. Nat said, "It did things to a man… to find out he had a brain." Explain. Do you agree?
2. Why did Nat lie for Lem? Were his actions justifiable?
3. How did learning change Lem's attitude? Why do you think it did?

Chapter 16

Review Questions
1. Why did Captain Prince repeatedly exclaim to Nat, "You *mathematician*!"?
2. Describe the outrigger canoe.
3. What happened on the return trip that made the crew short-handed?
4. What did it mean to have a ledge named for you?
5. Who was waiting for Nat when he reached the wharf? Why wasn't Nat pleased?

Thought Questions
1. How did Nat's feelings for Elizabeth change during this voyage? Why do you think he only realized how he felt when he was far from home?
2. Which do you think would be worse—a leak or a fight? Why? What is the difference between these two disasters and the responses they demand?
3. Does the age gap between Nat and Elizabeth seem significant to you? Why or why not? Do you think it was more or less significant in Nat's time than it would be today?

Chapter 17

Review Questions
1. Why did America need a navy?
2. How did Mr. Blunt respond to Nat's criticisms?

3. Why did David want Nat to be at the husking party?
4. What did a red ear of corn mean? What did Nat and Elizabeth decide to do?
5. Where did Captain Prince intend to sail next?
6. What news did the Harveys bring about Lem?
7. Why did Nat prefer the French to the English farewell?

Thought Questions
1. Was Nat an astronomer? What gives a title like that its worth and meaning?
2. Captain Prince told Elizabeth that, "An anchor won't hold if the cable's too short." What does this tell you about his definition of a proper mariner's wife? Do you agree?
3. Do women know more about love than men do? If so, why? Discuss.
4. Is "not worrying" more important than hearing the truth? Which would you prefer? Why? Compare this chapter's treatment of the question to the events in Chapter 5 (Thought Questions). Do you see a pattern?

Chapter 18

Review Questions
1. Why did Nat say he was going to check all the published figures and tables sailors used?
2. How did the Englishman at Cadiz tell Captain Prince to detect French spies?
3. Why did the Spanish health officer throw the logbook overboard?
4. Whom did Charlie suspect of being a spy?
5. What did the gunfire from the British fleet mean?
6. Why did Captain Prince leave the British convoy? What happened when the three French ships approached? Why didn't Nat realize the danger was over?
7. What news did Captain Gorman bring to Nat?

Thought Questions
1. How did Nat help Charlie avoid homesickness? What is the parallel between this incident and the one at the end of the chapter? What theme develops as a result?
2. Would you describe Nat as a "great scholar"? What does that title mean? Explain.
3. Do you agree with Captain Prince's advice about being completely honest with your spouse? Why or why not?
4. Does work help you deal with loss? Is it a permanent cure, or just a temporary one?

Chapter 19

Review Questions
1. How had Elizabeth died?
2. What was Elias Hasket Derby's last dream?
3. What honor did Nat receive from the American Academy of Arts and Sciences?
4. Where did Captain Prince ask Nat to sail with him?
5. What did Mr. Blunt ask Nat to do? Why did Nat agree?
6. Did Nat and Polly say goodbye? If so, how?
7. What had happened to the *Astrea*'s first crew?
8. How did Captain Prince keep the new crew from deserting?

Thought Questions
1. What is *consumption* called today? Is there a cure for it?

2. What does it mean to say someone can "see around corners"? How could you develop that skill?
3. Why did Polly leave a note to say goodbye? Do you think Americans place more emphasis on saying goodbye than on saying hello? Discuss.

Chapter 20

Review Questions
1. What did Lupe want from Nat? What did he offer in return? What did Nat have to do in order to fulfill Lupe's request?
2. How many errors did Nat find in Moore's tables? What did this work inspire him to do?
3. Why was the trip to Batavia a failure? What did Nat propose to do instead? What made the alternate destination so complicated?
4. Of what did the Harveys accuse Nat when he returned to Boston?
5. Why had the *Betsy* wrecked?
6. What had happened to Nat's brothers?

Thought Questions
1. Why did Nat say, "Lupe was the worst of the crew, because he smiled"? Why do you think Nat was so frightened of Lupe?
2. Is it better to use an advanced method that, if flawed, is more dangerous, but if accurate, is more reliable than the old way? Defend your position.

Chapter 21

Review Questions
1. How did Polly explain why Nat needed to write his book?
2. Why did Nat and Polly end their honeymoon early?
3. What did Captain Ingersoll and Captain Prince propose to do with the *John*?
4. What did Nat do with his book after it was accepted for publication?
5. What happened to the *John*?

Thought Questions
1. Was the sea at fault for all the sailors' deaths? Why did Lois blame the sea?
2. Would other countries be more likely to pay attention to an American book today? Why or why not? What has changed since Nat's time?

Chapter 22

Review Questions
1. What analogy did Dr. Holyoke make about book sailing? Did Nat think men were right to blame books for ships being lost?
2. Where was Nat's book published?
3. What was Nat's role on the *Putnam*?
4. What award did Nat receive from Harvard?
5. Who surprised Nat and Polly at their home? What had happened to him?

Thought Questions
1. Why do you think people find it easier to believe superstitions and doubt scientists? Are scientific explanations always correct? Discuss.
2. Why do prophets not receive honor in their own countries? Is this always the case?

3. Would you describe Nat as a prophet? Why or why not?
4. Why did Nat want to go to Commencement Day at Harvard? Why did he still want that recognition, even after all the things he had accomplished?

Chapter 23

Review Questions
1. Why couldn't Lem sail with the *Putnam*?
2. What kind of storm did the *Putnam* encounter?
3. Where did the *Putnam* find pepper? What difficulties did they run into?
4. Why wouldn't Nat let more than two Malays onto the ship at one time?
5. What factors made the trip home so difficult?

Thought Questions
1. How does Latham depict Malaysia and other international locations in this book? What impression does this book give of the people there? Is it respectful? Critical? Discuss.
2. What did Nat come to understand about Captain Prince after commanding his own ship?
3. What do you think makes fog so frightening?

Chapter 24

Review Questions
1. How did Nat know Chad's wake was straight?
2. What did Nat want to see through the fog?
3. How did Nat calm Corey as they passed Baker's Island?
4. Why, according to Lem, should Polly hope Nat did not come that night?
5. How long had Nat gone without shooting the sun?

Thought Questions
1. Which is more efficient in a fog, mathematics or traditional navigation? Explain. Is mathematics always reliable?
2. Did Polly trust Nat or the math he used? Explain. Is there a difference?
3. Did Nat ever not "sail by ash breeze"? If so, when?
4. Was Nat ever becalmed in life? If not, why not? What can you learn from his example?

Little Britches: Father and I Were Ranchers
Ralph Moody

Introduction

Ralph Moody (1898–1982), an American author, did not write a book until he was over fifty years old. His first book, *Little Britches: Father and I Were Ranchers*, is about his family's adventures moving from New Hampshire to a ranch in Colorado when he was eight years old. He went on to write eighteen more popular children's books about rural life in the early twentieth century.

Reading Practice: Note-taking

Remember, note-taking is not about copying what the book (or speaker) says word for word. Instead, it is about picking the most important information and putting it into your own words. To practice taking notes, read a chapter, set down the book, and write a few words to remind you of the main events or ideas. Use the Review Questions as needed to remind you of points you may have missed. Include examples of symbolism, important quotes, key descriptions, recurring themes, or even hints about events to come. You can use anything from note cards to a blank piece of paper or sticky notes to record your ideas.

Going Deeper: Character Development

Even though the characters in *Little Britches* are (auto)biographical, in telling his family's story, Moody had to turn his family members into characters with whom readers could sympathize. To do so, rather than giving a moment-by-moment account of their lives, he chose incidents and conversations that reveal specific character traits.

As you read, focus on the interactions between the characters. What lessons does Ralph hear from his parents? What lessons are unspoken? Pay attention to Ralph's reaction to the things he sees and experiences. Whose actions and ideas does he seem to mimic? Look for places where Ralph embraces a new idea or comes to some realization. Because he is writing about himself, Moody could have told readers, "That's when I changed my mind about X." Instead, because this is a story, not an autobiography, try to notice how Moody develops his own character through both his experiences and his relationships with other people.

Chapter 1

Review Questions
1. Who was Cousin Phil?
2. Why did Ralph's family move to Colorado?
3. Did the ranch meet Mother's expectations? Why or why not?
4. What happened to Bill and Nig?

Thought Questions
1. Why do you think Mother and Father reacted differently to the sight of their new house? What do their reactions tell you about their characters?
2. Father told Ralph, "If you just remember to measure twice and saw once, you'll get along all right." Can you apply that lesson to other situations?
3. How did Ralph respond to the horses' accident? How did Father respond? What does Father's response suggest about the traits he values?
4. Father told Ralph "it's that sort of thing that makes a fellow into a man." Do you agree? Discuss.

Chapter 2

Review Questions
1. How were Fred, Bessie, and Mrs. Aultland related to each other?
2. What newspaper article frightened Mother?
3. Why did Father take a lantern out to the barn in the middle of the night?
4. What did the Moodys mistake for a mountain lion?
5. Describe the neighbors who came to visit.

Thought Questions
1. Why do you think Father refused Fred Aultland's offer of horses? When do you think it's okay, or even wise, to accept help?
2. Father said, "We'll have to face the situations we find in this country." Was he trying to comfort Mother? If not, what do you think he was trying to tell her?
3. How does Ralph describe the new neighbors? What does his description tell you about his first impression of them?

Chapter 3

Review Questions
1. Who made Ralph's life miserable at school?
2. Why didn't Ralph fight back?
3. How and why did Ralph exaggerate the effects of the cold?
4. How did Ralph finally resolve his conflicts at school?

Thought Questions
1. Do you agree with Mother's argument against fighting?
2. Grace adjusted to school by teaching the girls a new game; Ralph had to adjust by fighting. What does that tell you about the expectations for boys and girls? Do you think those expectations were a good thing? Why or why not?
3. At the end of the chapter, Father affirms what Mother had punished. How does Ralph present the situation? Do you think Mother and Father handled it well? Discuss.

Chapter 4

Review Questions

1. Who helped Ralph fight Freddie?
2. What new nickname did Ralph earn? Who gave it to him?
3. Why did Ralph lie to Mother and Grace about the crossties?
4. How did Father punish Ralph?

Thought Questions

1. Explain Father's comparison of a man's character to his house. Do you agree?
2. What makes punishment effective? What is the purpose of punishment?
3. Do you think you can permanently damage your character? Why or why not? (Begin by defining what you mean by *character*.)

Chapter 5

Review Questions

1. Why did Mother begin holding Sunday services at home?
2. How did the Moodys stay safe during the big wind? Where did they go?
3. Why did Mother prevent Father from going to look for the horses?

Thought Questions

1. Why do you think Mother cried over little things, but not over the destruction of the house? How does her response to tragedy differ from Father's? Does she demonstrate a different kind of strength?
2. What words would you use to describe Mother's and Father's characters at this point in the book?

Chapter 6

Review Questions

1. Who was Mr. Wright? What offer did he make to Father?
2. What did Father receive in payment for his work?
3. What went wrong when Father tried to plow the garden?
4. What problem with the land had Cousin Phil not mentioned to Father?

Thought Questions

1. Why do you think Moody spends so much time describing Father's attempts to train Fanny to plow? What does this incident reveal about his character?
2. Fred said, "I won't steal water from you, Charlie, but when only half my own is coming through to me and my crop's suffering, I won't pass it on to you." Should people always be generous, even if it means going without something they need?

Chapter 7

Review Questions

1. Who stopped to visit while Mother was planting the garden?
2. Why didn't the horse turn left when Ralph pulled on the left rein?
3. According to Father, what made Hi a good horseman?
4. How did Ralph finally manage to ride Fanny? What was the result?

Thought Questions

1. Why does hearing someone say "I'm proud of you" have so much impact?

2. What is the difference between reading and "talking a book"? Can you learn to read that way? If so, how?
3. Do you think Ralph should have been punished for riding Fanny? Do you agree with Father's approach? Why or why not?

Chapter 8

Review Questions
1. What job did Mrs. Corcoran hire Ralph to do?
2. Why did Ralph find the job more difficult than he had imagined?
3. How did Grace try to convince Mother to let Ralph work on Sundays?

Thought Questions
1. What was your first job? Do you think Ralph's was a job for a boy or a man?
2. Are there still stereotypes about being "city-raised" or "country-raised"? If not, what stereotypes have taken their place? Is that kind of generalization based on truth?

Chapter 9

Review Questions
1. What did Ralph discover about Fanny the first day he rode her to herd the cows?
2. What went wrong the first time Grace tried to ride Fanny?
3. Why was Father upset with Ralph when he got home that night?
4. How did Grace convince Ralph to let her ride Fanny every day?

Thought Questions
1. What was the difference between playing cowboy and being a good cowboy? Can you think of other examples in which the fun part of a job is not the most important?
2. Father said, "The least government is the best government." Do you agree? Discuss.
3. Grace used "her conscience" to manipulate Ralph into letting her ride the horse. Why do you think she did that? Was she really following her conscience?
4. Do you think Grace was wise or a sissy because she wouldn't fall off of Fanny? Explain.
5. Why did Ralph put the quarter in his overall pocket while he was riding home, even if no one could see it?

Chapter 10

Review Questions
1. Who was Two Dog?
2. Why had he and Mr. Thompson come to see the Moodys?
3. Why were Two Dog and Mr. Thompson blood brothers?
4. How did Ralph communicate with Two Dog?
5. What did Mrs. Corcoran tell Ralph about Mr. Thompson and Two Dog?

Thought Questions
1. How did Ralph feel about Two Dog? Why do you think he felt that way? How do you respond to people who are different from you?

    2. How did Father say Ralph could prove that Mr. Thompson's stories were true? Do you use the same method to resolve arguments? If not, why not?

Chapter 11

Review Questions
1. How did Father modify Fred's hay stacker to make the work easier for the men?
2. What was Ralph's favorite part of the work day?
3. Why did Jerry Alder fight with the young man from Denver?
4. What dampened Ralph's excitement about the paycheck when he and Father got home?

Thought Questions
1. How was Jerry Alder's fight with the man from Denver different from Ralph's fight with Freddie Sprague? What does this book imply about using physical force to resolve conflict? Do you agree?
2. Compare Ralph's unwillingness to ride pickaback home from the Aultlands' with his desire to carry the quarter from the Corcorans'. What do these two incidents tell you about his character?

Chapter 12

Review Questions
1. Why did Ralph go to get Two Dog?
2. Why did the journey take longer than he had expected?
3. How had Mr. Thompson known Ralph was coming?
4. How did Father and Mother respond when Mr. Thompson and Two Dog brought Ralph home?
5. What happened to Bill in the morning?

Thought Questions
1. Why did Ralph think Two Dog would know how to heal Bill? What special abilities did Two Dog have? How do you think he got them?
2. Even though Ralph's intentions were good, was it right for him to seek help on his own? Discuss.

Chapter 13

Review Questions
1. What did Father and Mother hope to buy at the auction?
2. How did Fred Aultland help them get the animals they wanted?
3. Why was Mother flustered on the ride home?

Thought Questions
1. Do you think Fred's behavior at the auction was right? Why or why not? What does the book's tone imply about the scene?
2. What do you learn about Fred's and Mrs. Corcoran's personalities from this chapter?

Chapter 14

Review Questions
1. What was the irrigation fight about?

2.   Why would going to the law not guarantee the ranchers their fair share of water?

3.   How did the ranchers at the tail of the ditch decide to get their water?

4.   At the meeting Saturday night, what did Father suggest they do? Did it work?

Thought Questions

1.   Fred said the only way to get justice was "to take the law into our own hands." Do you agree? What might be the consequences of that choice?

2.   Father said, "There are times a man has to do things he doesn't like to, in order to protect his family." Discuss. How would you decide when distasteful things were necessary?

3.   To get the water, Father was willing to fight, but given the choice, he chose to negotiate. What does this tell you about his character? Can you learn something from his actions?

Chapter 15

Review Questions

1.   Why did Ralph stop herding Mrs. Corcoran's cows?

2.   Who was Mr. Lake? Why did Ralph and Grace get in trouble with him?

3.   What was the incident with the cellar door?

4.   How did Ralph lose his glasses?

Thought Questions

1.   Do you think Mr. Lake deserved what he got? Why or why not?

2.   Was Ralph proud of "losing" his glasses? What does this incident, and the way he describes it, tell you about his character?

Chapter 16

Review Questions

1.   How did Bill die? How did Father get a new horse?

2.   Describe Father's method for training the colt to pull.

3.   Why did Father need poles to build a cellar?

Thought Questions

1.   Mother and Father did practical arithmetic while Grace and Ralph were doing their homework. Do you think that had an effect on the way Ralph thought about school? What influences people's attitudes toward learning?

2.   Father said, "The only time to feel sorry for anything—or anybody—that dies is when they haven't completed their mission here on earth." Do you agree? Is there a difference between mourning someone's death and feeling sorry for the one who died?

Chapter 17

Review Questions

1.   For what did Father need the hardware and iron?

2.   What did Ralph catch in his trap?

3.   When Ralph confessed what he had done, how did the sheriff respond?

4.   What did Father bring back with him after spending the day with Fred?

Thought Questions

1. Why do you think people run away from the law, even if running away is a worse crime than the one they committed first?
2. Why did Ralph want advice only after he got in trouble? Do you ever do the same thing?
3. Is it true that "a man always [makes] his troubles less by going to meet them instead of waiting for them to catch up with him, or trying to run away from them"?

Chapter 18

Review Questions

1. What did Ralph do to fulfill his craving for chocolate?
2. Which lines from Shakespeare kept unsettling Ralph's plans?
3. What happened when Ralph tried to cut off a piece of the chocolate?
4. What did Father say that hurt worse than the spanking?

Thought Questions

1. How did Ralph misinterpret Father's lesson about facing up to your troubles?
2. Look at the way Ralph justifies his theft while he is going out to get the cows. How does your mind rationalize wrong choices you have made?
3. Discuss Ralph's use of the seed pods to "leave the whole matter to the Lord." Is that what he was really doing?

Chapter 19

Review Questions

1. Why were Father and Mother disappointed by the bean crop?
2. How did Ralph persuade Father to let him trap the pheasants?
3. What did Ralph name the new horse?

Thought Questions

1. Do you think Ralph violated the spirit of the law by catching the pheasants? Who decides what the spirit of the law is?
2. Do Ralph's choices in the situation with the pheasants show a change in his character from the way he handled the chocolate? Discuss.

Chapter 20

Review Questions

1. Describe the Moodys' Thanksgiving.
2. What happened right before Christmas? Why didn't Ralph like to remember it?
3. How did Father's box system work to divide up the water?
4. How did the gold panic affect the ranchers?

Thought Questions

1. Can you force someone to be honest? If not, why did a water system like Father's work?
2. Does money—or gold—have any innate value? What gives it value? Why do you think problems with the monetary system have such a big impact?

Chapter 21

Review Questions

1. What went wrong when Ralph was raking the hay?
2. What had prevented his tenth toe from breaking?
3. Who was Lucy? What new things did she tell Ralph?
4. How did Father react when Ralph told him what Lucy had said?

Thought Questions

1. Can you think of an example in which a minor injury or disappointment (like the stone bruise) protected you from greater danger? What lesson could you take from this incident?
2. Lucy told Ralph, "the world owed them a living." How would you respond?
3. Do you agree with Father that the only two kinds of men in the world are honest and dishonest ones? Can you tell the difference right away? If so, how?

Chapter 22

Review Questions

1. Why did Mother and Father invite Ralph to help them plan the family budget?
2. How had Cousin Phil changed when Ralph saw him in his Denver office?
3. Why was Father able to purchase more items in Denver than he had planned?
4. Describe some of the ways the Moodys handled their resources wisely during the panic.

Thought Questions

1. Why was someone like Cousin Phil affected more severely by the panic than Ralph and his family were?
2. Were Ralph and his family rich? Is wealth measured only in money?
3. Why do you think Ralph loved Father more after Father scolded him?

Chapter 23

Review Questions

1. What did Ralph's family do when the tornado came?
2. What happened to Fanny and Ralph when Ralph was trying to beat the cloudburst?

Thought Questions

1. What does Ralph's response to the accident tell you about his character development? Contrast his response in this situation to his reaction to earlier incidents.

Chapter 24

Review Questions

1. What kind of job did Mr. Cooper offer Ralph?
2. What had Hi made for Ralph?
3. Which horse did Ralph want to ride? Why was Mr. Cooper reluctant to let him try?
4. Describe Hi's method for gentle-breaking the blue colt.

Thought Questions

1. How did Ralph respond to his fear of riding the new horse? When is it wise to ignore your fears, and when do you think you should listen to them?

Chapter 25

Review Questions

1. What did Ralph name the colt?
2. What was Ralph's job with the chuck wagon?
3. What advice did Father give Ralph before he returned to the ranch on Sunday night?

Thought Questions

1. If you are surrounded by people who swear or use coarse language, are you more likely to imitate them? What would prevent that from happening?
2. Ralph thought Grace wished she were a boy. Do you think boys were given more privileges? If so, why? Did they also have more responsibility?
3. Explain Father's comparison of a man's life to a boat. Why do you think he told Ralph that particular story at that time? What point was he trying to make?

Chapter 26

Review Questions

1. What did Ralph learn during his six weeks at the mountain ranch?
2. What were Sky High's two faults? How did Hi fix them?

Thought Questions

1. Do you think Hi's methods for training Sky High were cruel? Did they work? Discuss.
2. Hi said, "The lessons you remember longest are the ones that hurt you the most when you learn 'em." Is the same thing true for you? Why or why not?

Chapter 27

Review Questions

1. What had caused the Bear Creek ditch fight? Why was Father in danger?
2. How did Hi trick Father into keeping the gun and learning to shoot it?
3. What did Father tell Ralph as he was leaving to go back to the mountains?

Thought Questions

1. Is there a connection between training boys and schooling horses? If so, what is it?
2. Do you agree with Ralph that "sometimes it's nicer not to talk when you're near somebody you love"? What makes silence pleasant or uncomfortable?
3. Do you think the relationship between Ralph and Father has changed at this point in the story? If so, how?

Chapter 28

Review Questions

1. Describe the Fourth of July roundup. What did Ralph do to participate?
2. What stunts did Ralph learn to do with Hi? When did he want to perform?
3. What was in the box Bill Engle had left for Ralph?
4. What were the results of the trick riding competition?

Thought Questions

1. Was Ralph dishonest with his family about the trick riding stunts he was planning to do? How was this secret different than the incident with the chocolate?

Chapter 29

Review Questions

   1.   How was Father going to prove in court how much water had been stolen?

   2.   What happened when the horseless carriage drove past the house?

   3.   How did Ralph find out that Billy and Brindle were missing? What had happened to them?

Thought Questions

   1.   Was it giving up for Father to say they wouldn't make it on the ranch? When is it wise to admit defeat?

   2.   Father said, "There's always a living in this world for the fellow who's willing to work for it." Do you agree? Discuss.

   3.   Do you think Father should have accepted help from the neighbors? Why or why not?

Chapter 30

Review Questions

   1.   To what new location did the Moody family move?

   2.   Why did Ralph get into trouble at the new school?

   3.   How did Father respond to Ralph's punishment?

   4.   What did Father promise Ralph after he finished his house?

Thought Questions

   1.   Explain the quote from Hamlet: "There's a divinity that shapes our ends, rough hew them how we will." Discuss.

   2.   How would you respond if you received punishment for doing the right thing? Is there a right way to react?

   3.   Did Father's response surprise you? Compare his handling of the situation to the way he responded to the shooters in Chapter 29 and the water thieves in Chapter 14. What patterns do you notice in his behavior?

Chapter 31

Review Questions

   1.   What happened to Father when he took Babe up to Fort Logan? How did the accident affect his health?

   2.   What did Father tell the children about his boyhood?

   3.   Why were the children sent to different homes after school? What had happened?

   4.   Why did Mother have to go to the hospital?

   5.   How did Ralph know he had become a man?

Thought Questions

   1.   Do you think Father knew he was ill when he gathered the children to talk about his childhood? Why do you think he wanted them to know about his past?

   2.   Discuss your response to the end of the story. Why do you think Moody chose to end the way he did?

   3.   What is the difference between a boy and a man? A girl and a woman? What produces that change? How did Ralph change over the course of the book?

The Lion, the Witch and the Wardrobe
C. S. Lewis

Introduction

The Lion, the Witch and the Wardrobe is the best-known of C. S. Lewis' *Chronicles of Narnia* series. It was published in 1950 and has remained a favorite of children and adults ever since. The book shows Lewis' mastery of presenting old stories in a new and fantastical setting, giving readers a new perspective on familiar themes (in this case, the biblical message of salvation).

Reading Practice: Maps

Look at several different types of maps: road maps, topographic maps, political maps, physical maps, climate maps, and resource or economic maps. Which types might be relevant or helpful for this book?

Draw a map of Narnia as the Pevensie children find it. Now contrast this map to the one you drew when you read *The Magician's Nephew*. What physical changes took place in Narnia between Digory's departure and Lucy's arrival? In a larger sense, think about the way the Narnia series links physical changes to political, social, or moral changes.

Going Deeper: Genre

The Lion, the Witch and the Wardrobe is a good example of the influence genre may have on a book's symbolism. As a fantasy novel, the story takes place in another world, one which, though it shares some characteristics with the real world, comes from Lewis's imagination. Even though writing fantasy gives authors an enormous amount of creative freedom, the genre comes with its own set of challenges. Because the setting is imaginary and may include things that don't exist in the real world, the moral of the story may not apply to you exactly as written. Part of reading a fantasy novel is translating the big ideas from the author's imaginary world to your own.

As you read, notice the structure of Narnia. What are the rules? What are the sources of power? Look back at the questions about magic in *The Magician's Nephew* and *The Secret Garden*, and consider whether or not the same questions apply to this book. Compare the problems the Pevensies face in the real world to the ones they encounter in Narnia. How, if at all, are the two worlds similar? When you encounter a character, an object, or an incident that seems to symbolize a bigger idea, ask yourself how you might represent the same idea in your world.

Chapter 1

Review Questions
1. Why were the four children sent away from London? Where were they sent?
2. What did Lucy find in the wardrobe?
3. What was a Faun?

Thought Questions
1. Was it kind to send children away from their families just to keep them safe? If you were sent away from home, what would your response be? Do you think you would act like Lucy, Edmund, Peter, or Susan?
2. If you were going to create an imaginary world, how would you begin? What questions would you have to ask?

Chapter 2

Review Questions
1. What was a "Daughter of Eve"?
2. From what country did Mr. Tumnus think Lucy came? Why did he think that?
3. Why was it always winter in Narnia?
4. What orders had the White Witch given to Mr. Tumnus?
5. What did Lucy give Mr. Tumnus before they parted?

Thought Questions
1. Why do you think Lewis had the Narnians refer to humans as Sons of Adam and Daughters of Eve? What is the effect of linking Narnia to biblical history?
2. Was Mr. Tumnus a nice Faun? Why or why not? On what did you base your answer?
3. Do you think it is easier or harder to be cruel to people you know? Why?
4. If the White Witch made the laws of Narnia, would Mr. Tumnus have been justified in following them? Why or why not? When, if ever, is it okay to break the law?

Chapter 3

Review Questions
1. Why hadn't Lucy's brothers and sister worried about her absence?
2. Why didn't the other children believe in Narnia?
3. How did Edmund get into Narnia?
4. Whom did he meet in the woods?

Thought Questions
1. What do the children's responses to Lucy's explanation tell you about their characters?
2. Have you ever told a lie because it was easier than standing up for the truth? Explain.

Chapter 4

Review Questions
1. What did Edmund like best to eat?
2. In what part of Edmund's stories was the Queen most interested?
3. How did the Queen convince Edmund to bring his family to see her?
4. Who was the Queen, according to Lucy?

Thought Questions
1. What is your favorite food? What would you do to get it? Can good food or presents make you forget to be cautious? What does this suggest about human nature?
2. Mr. Tumnus and Lucy called the lady the White Witch, but Edmund met her as the Queen of Narnia. Does this difference in names excuse Edmund's choice to believe her?
3. Look at Chapters 4 and 5 of *The Magician's Nephew*. Compare Edmund's and Lucy's impressions of the White Witch to Digory's and Polly's views of Jadis.

Chapter 5

Review Questions
1. Why did Peter become angry at Edmund?
2. Whom did Peter and Susan tell about Lucy's strange behavior? What three answers did he offer? What was his advice?
3. Why did the four children have to hide in the wardrobe?

Thought Questions
1. Why do you think Edmund lied about getting into Narnia?
2. Is it harder to trust someone who has told lies before? Can a person ever win back the trust of others after breaking it?
3. If you were in Peter and Susan's place, which of the professor's three answers would you be most likely to believe. Why?
4. If possible, read in *Mere Christianity* Lewis's "trilemma" about Jesus' identity ("Lord, liar, or lunatic"). Compare this argument to the professor's description of Lucy. Why do you think Lewis used such similar arguments for such (seemingly) different situations?

Chapter 6

Review Questions
1. How did Edmund give away the fact that he had already visited Narnia?
2. What did the children find at Mr. Tumnus's cave?
3. Who led the children away from the cave?

Thought Questions
1. Would it have been wrong for the children to go home and leave Mr. Tumnus to his fate? Why or why not? What made them responsible for him?
2. How could the children be certain that it was the Queen, not Mr. Tumnus, who was evil? Why do you think they believed his side of the story?

Chapter 7

Review Questions
1. What kind of animal did the children see in the trees? Why was it spying on them?
2. What did the children feel when the beaver said Aslan was on the move?
3. What did Edmund notice while the rest were looking at Mr. Beaver's house?

Thought Questions
1. Why did the children decide to trust the beaver? In their position, would you have followed him? How would you decide?

2. When you read about the Beavers, is it hard to remember they are not humans? Can you tell that they are animals from the way they are described? If so, how? What purpose do you think it serves for Lewis to use talking animals in Narnia?

3. In several places, Lewis describes in detail the food the children eat. What is the effect on the story? On the way you perceive Narnia? Discuss.

Chapter 8

Review Questions

1. Who had taken Mr. Tumnus? Where did they take him?
2. Who was Aslan? Where were the children supposed to meet him?
3. Was the Witch human?
4. Did the children and the Beavers find Edmund? Why did Mr. Beaver say they should stop looking?

Thought Questions

1. Does Aslan sound safe?
2. Mr. Beaver said of Aslan, "Who said anything about safe? 'Course he isn't safe. But he's good. He's the King, I tell you." Is this reassuring? Can you think of other examples of things that are good but not safe?
3. Discuss Mr. Beaver's account of the Queen's history, especially the connection to the book of Genesis. Why do you think Lewis created this link to biblical history?

Chapter 9

Review Questions

1. When had Edmund left the Beavers' house? How much did he hear?
2. What did Edmund do to the stone lion in the courtyard?
3. What happened when Edmund reached the threshold?

Thought Questions

1. Why do you think Edmund stopped jeering at the stone lion? What does a noble face look like? Does it have specific characteristics?
2. Do you think Edmund heard the wolf add "or else not so fortunate" when he welcomed Edmund? Do you think he would have responded to the comment if he had heard it?

Chapter 10

Review Questions

1. Was Mrs. Beaver pessimistic about their chances? Why or why not?
2. Why did Mr. Beaver scamper out of the hole in the bank when he heard sleigh bells?
3. What indicated to Mr. Beaver that the Witch's power was crumbling?
4. What did Father Christmas give to each of the children?

Thought Questions

1. How was Father Christmas different from other wintry things? Why had the Witch kept him out? What is the source of Father Christmas and Santa Claus stories? Why do you think Lewis uses this familiar figure as a symbol of goodness in Narnia?

2. Father Christmas said that "battles are ugly when women fight." What does this tell you about his view of women? Of war? Explain. Do you agree?

Chapter 11

Review Questions
1. Did the Witch reward Edmund for his information?
2. What was the group of animals doing that caused the Witch to stop the sledge?
3. Why did the Witch slap Edmund?
4. Why did she have to abandon her sledge?

Thought Questions
1. What did it take for Edmund to believe that the Witch was evil? Why do you think he refused to believe it earlier?
2. Why did Edmund feel sorry for the animals? What does this tell you about his character?
3. What causes repentance? Why do you think small incidents sometimes have a greater impact on your conscience than big events do?

Chapter 12

Review Questions
1. What did it mean when springtime suddenly appeared in Narnia?
2. What was Aslan's response when he found out Edmund had become a traitor?
3. What was the name of the castle that Aslan showed to Peter? Why was the castle significant for Peter and his siblings?
4. Why did Susan blow her horn?
5. What new name did Peter earn?

Thought Questions
1. Can something be good and terrible at the same time? Give an example.
2. Did Aslan blame Peter for Edmund's betrayal? Why or why not? Was it his fault?
3. What does Peter's battle with the wolf tell you about his character?
4. Why did Aslan remind Peter to clean his sword? What might a clean sword symbolize?

Chapter 13

Review Questions
1. Why did the Witch want to kill Edmund? What prevented her?
2. How did the dwarf and the Witch escape?
3. What was the Deep Magic? Why was Aslan unable to ignore it?

Thought Questions
1. How were the creatures the Witch called allies different from Aslan's allies?
2. What do you think Aslan said to Edmund when they were alone?
3. Why did Aslan and the Witch present such a contrast when they stood next to each other? Is the difference between good and evil always easy to see?
4. Discuss the concept of the Deep Magic. Can you think of a comparable set of laws in the real world, with a similar penalty for breaking them?
5. Who or what do you think the Emperor-beyond-the-Sea symbolizes? What about Aslan? The White Witch?

6. Why do you think the Witch believed Aslan's promise after he roared? If his roar had contained words, what do you think it would have said to her?

Chapter 14

Review Questions
1. Why were Susan and Lucy unable to sleep that night?
2. What was wrong with Aslan?
3. What did the children see at the Stone Table?
4. Why were Aslan's enemies less afraid of him after he had been shaved?
5. What did the Witch say to Aslan before she killed him? Why did she think she had won?

Thought Questions
1. Why did the Witch call Aslan a fool?
2. How is the scene of Aslan's death similar to Jesus' crucifixion (see Matthew 26–27)? How is it different? Does a fictional story need to be exactly the same as a true one in order to contain truth? Also, think about this question in relation to some of the historical fiction novels you have read.

Chapter 15

Review Questions
1. Where did the Witch go when she left the Stone Table?
2. What did the mice do to Aslan?
3. What did Susan and Lucy hear as they were looking at Cair Paravel?
4. What happened to the Stone Table?
5. How did the children know Aslan was not a ghost?
6. How did Aslan get into the Witch's castle?

Thought Questions
1. If you had been in Susan and Lucy's place, would you think Aslan had died for nothing?
2. Susan asked, "What does it all mean?" Discuss Aslan's answer about the deeper magic. How does it relate to the idea of sacrifice? How does it relate to Christianity?
3. Does it seem strange to hear the description of the children playing with Aslan? Think back to the description of Aslan as "good, but not safe" (Chapter 8). How does this scene fit into that characterization?

Chapter 16

Review Questions
1. What did Aslan do to the statues?
2. Whom did Lucy find in the Witch's castle?
3. Describe what Lucy saw on the battlefield.

Thought Questions
1. Aslan said, "Once the feet are put right, all the rest of him will follow." Do you think he was just talking about the statue, or was it symbolic of a bigger idea? If so, what?
2. Is it fitting that Aslan was the one to kill the Witch? Could anyone else have killed her?

3. Lewis's description of the battle scene is relatively brief. What does that tell you about the main point of the story? Why do you think the battle was less important?

Chapter 17

Review Questions
1. Who had turned the tide of the battle before Aslan arrived? How?
2. How did Lucy save Edmund?
3. Who left during the celebration of the children's coronation?
4. What names did the children earn as they grew older? What do those names tell you about how their characters had changed?
5. What did the four kings and queens find in the thicket when they were hunting?
6. Why did the children feel they must tell the professor about their adventures?
7. Was Narnia gone forever, according to the professor?

Thought Questions
1. Why do you think Peter looked different after the battle? Why do people change when they are faced with heavy responsibilities?
2. Do you think Edmund should have been told what Aslan did for him? Why or why not?
3. Why do you think Aslan left?
4. Discuss the relationship between this story and the story of Christ. Do you think this story is a perfect re-telling of the gospel? Why or why not? What are the advantages and limitations of using fantasy stories to talk about God?

The Hiding Place
Corrie ten Boom

Introduction

Corrie ten Boom (1892–1983) lived in the Netherlands during the Holocaust. In an example of supreme courage, Corrie and her family worked to shelter Jews from the Nazis. As a result, Corrie and several family members spent time in various concentration camps around Europe. Even after her release, Corrie spent time working to restore and revive the survivors of the Holocaust, oppressors and oppressed alike. Corrie's story, entitled *The Hiding Place*, was written in 1971 with the help of John and Elizabeth Sherrill.

Reading Practice: Note-taking

Remember, note-taking is not about copying what the book (or speaker) says word for word. Instead, it is about picking the most important information and putting it into your own words. To practice taking notes, read a chapter, set down the book, and write a few words to remind you of the main events or ideas. Use the Review Questions as needed to remind you of points you may have missed. Include examples of symbolism, important quotes, key descriptions, recurring themes, or even hints about events to come. You can use anything from note cards to a blank piece of paper or sticky notes to record your ideas.

Going Deeper: Themes

As you have seen, authors sometimes use minor events, characters, or problems (sub-plots), to reflect or emphasize the main plot. Even though *The Hiding Place* tells the story of a real family's struggles and victories, it was written after the fact, and the incidents and details included were chosen because they work together to form a cohesive story.

As you read, ask yourself what the situations that confront Corrie have in common. Think about the way she handles difficult situations and how she confronts evil. How do Corrie's memories of her earlier childhood relate to the challenges she and her family faced in the concentration camps? Using your notes, try to identify the main themes of the book, and pay special attention to the way Corrie's faith in God shapes and directs her story.

Chapter 1

Review Questions
1. How old was Corrie at the beginning of the book?
2. Why did Betsie and Corrie nickname Mr. Sluring "Pickwick"?
3. What did the people of the city call Father?
4. Who was Christoffels? Why was he late?
5. What was Father's secret?
6. Why did Corrie worry about Willem?
7. Who arrived at the party with him? Why did the newcomer cause a stir?

Thought Questions
1. Corrie asked, "If I had known [what was to come] would I have gone ahead? Could I have done the things I did?" Do you think this is why God does not always reveal his plans in advance?
2. How valuable is business sense? Is it the most important thing in terms of running a business? What else might be equally important?
3. Explain Corrie's quote, "Memories are the key not to the past, but to the future." Do you agree? Why is it necessary to remember the past in order to move forward? Does the same thing apply to past tragedies? Keep this question in mind as you continue the book.

Chapter 2

Review Questions
1. What age was Corrie in this chapter?
2. Why couldn't Betsie play with the other children?
3. Who took Corrie to school?
4. Why did Father travel to Amsterdam? What did Corrie ask Father on the way home? How did he respond?
5. How did Corrie's family get to listen to the concerts without tickets?
6. What happened to make Corrie afraid of death? How did Father comfort her?

Thought Questions
1. Tante Jans believed that "our welfare in the hereafter depended on how much we could accomplish here on earth." Do you agree? Discuss.
2. Does the description of Father's self-education (five languages, theology, history, etc.) surprise you? What does this tell you about the different standard of learning in his time?
3. Corrie said "fear is never funny." Have you ever made fun of someone for their fears?
4. How did Father answer Corrie's question about *sex sin*? What does his answer tell you about his character? How did Father's answer compare to the way God sometimes answers prayer?
5. Why do you think "a society which hid the facts of sex from children made no effort to shield them from death"? Was death more common in that time? How are children (and adults) taught to think about death today?

Chapter 3

Review Questions
1. Who was Karel?

2. What did Corrie do after she finished secondary school?
3. What was wrong with Tante Jans? How did she respond to the test results in January?
4. What event took the family down to Brabant in southern Holland?
5. What was the theme for Willem's first sermon?
6. Why did Willem caution Corrie not to love Karel?
7. Who arrived with Karel on a November afternoon?
8. What is the strongest force in the world, according to Father? How did he advise Corrie to deal with her lost love?

Thought Questions
1. Mama said, "[Happiness] is something we make inside ourselves." Do you agree? Is it possible to be cheerful even in very bad circumstances? Have you ever had to do that?
2. Explain Corrie's comment, "It was Father's train ticket, given at the moment itself." (See Chapter 2).
3. Why do you think the people of Holland did not want to hear about the war?
4. Do you think it is okay to marry for money? Why or why not?
5. Are there "right" words to say to someone who is hurting? Explain your answer.

Chapter 4

Review Questions
1. What happened to Mama? What lesson did Corrie learn from Mama's paralysis?
2. Why was Mama unhappy the night before Nollie's wedding?
3. What was the great miracle of Nollie's wedding day?
4. What did Corrie discover when she took over Betsie's job as Father's bookkeeper?
5. What did Betsie's illness help Betsie and Corrie realize?
6. What changes did the radio bring to the Ten Booms?
7. How did what the Ten Booms called a "German problem" finally affect the family?

Thought Questions
1. Does it seem odd that Mama wore black at her daughter's wedding? Think about cultural traditions in American weddings. How might these be different elsewhere?
2. Has God ever given you the strength to bear something otherwise unbearable? Explain. Is it necessary to reach the end of your own strength to recognize God's hand?
3. Why is the news such a powerful (and dangerous) force?
4. Is it hard to believe the Ten Booms forgot about the problem in Germany? Why? What were the Americans doing about Germany at this point in history (1939)?

Chapter 5

Review Questions
1. Why were the Ten Booms so eager to hear the Prime Minister's speech?
2. When did Corrie tell a conscious lie for the first time?
3. What were the hardest adjustments for the Ten Booms under the German occupation?
4. What were Dutch people who supported the Germans called?
5. How did they get this name?
6. When Father and Corrie watched the public arrest, why did Father surprise Corrie?

7. What happened to the Weil's Furrier?
8. What was The Bulldog's real name? What happened to his dogs?
9. What small incident changed Corrie's outlook on what was happening to the Jews?

Thought Questions
1. Is it possible to be totally neutral in a widespread war?
2. What does it mean to "base faith upon wishes"? Do you think Father was being realistic or pessimistic when he said Holland would fall? Explain. What is the difference?
3. Was Father talking about a literal battle when he said, "Holland's battle has just begun"?
4. Do you think you would have had the courage to stand up to the Germans? How does taking a stand as an individual differ from taking a stand as a nation? Look back at Chapter 2 of *The Lion, The Witch and the Wardrobe* (Thought Questions). Do you see a theme?
5. Corrie asked, "How should a Christian act when evil [is] in power?" How would you respond to her question?
6. Why did Mr. de Vries describe himself as a "completed Jew"?

Chapter 6

Review Questions
1. What happened at the end of the church service to draw the congregation to its feet? What was the result of Peter's defiance?
2. How did Mrs. Kleermaker hear about the Ten Booms?
3. How did Corrie get ration cards for the Jews hiding in the Beje?
4. In what way did Corrie's "watchmaker hands" come in handy?
5. Why did Mr. Smit like the Ten Booms' house so much?

Thought Questions
1. Why do you think Germany outlawed the Dutch national anthem? Why are anthems powerful? Was Peter's defiance meaningless?
2. Is it ever ethical to steal? Explain your answer.
3. Do you think it was wise for the Ten Booms to trust so many people with their secret? Was there another way they could have handled the situation? Did the Holocaust destroy individuals' ability to trust each other? If so, how?
4. Did you ever want a secret room when you were younger? What would it be like to need one?

Chapter 7

Review Questions
1. What was *the razzia*?
2. What was wrong with the hiding place in Nollie's house? Why did Nollie's training of her children put the men in danger?
3. Why was Mrs. DeBoer's house raided?
4. Why did Corrie give Mietje the corner of a bank note?
5. Interpret this line: "We have a man's watch here that's giving us trouble [...] the face is very old-fashioned."
6. Explain Eusie's joke about the 166th Psalm.
7. What did Pickwick scold Corrie for forgetting to do?

Thought Questions
1. Do you think God holds people to different standards when they are dealing with evil? Discuss.
2. Are lying by word and by deed equally bad? If not, which one do you think is worse?
3. How would you answer Corrie's question, "How would God Himself show truth and love at the same time in a world like this?"
4. Why did the pastor refuse to hide the Jewish baby? What factors might have influenced his choice?
5. What is "kosher" food? What is its purpose? Discuss this concept with your family.

Chapter 8

Review Questions
1. When was the most dangerous time of day in the Beje?
2. Why did old Katrien say Nollie had gone mad? What had she done?
3. Why did Rolf and the others burst into Corrie's room in the middle of the night?
4. In January, what did the police chief call Corrie into his office to ask?
5. Who was the first to be captured? How did it happen?

Thought Questions
1. Did Nollie betray Annaliese? Do you think she was obeying God? Think carefully before you answer.
2. Was the window washer a spy? What would it be like having to distrust everyone?
3. If Corrie could justify lying in defense of the Jews, why could she not justify killing? Is it possible to bend some rules and be strict about others without being hypocritical?
4. Why didn't the Ten Booms stop their work when it seemed they would be discovered?

Chapter 9

Review Questions
1. What day did the raid happen? Who betrayed them?
2. Why did Corrie have to leave her prison bag behind?
3. What made Kapteyn stop hitting Corrie?
4. Did the Germans find the secret room?
5. How many people were arrested from the Beje?

Thought Questions
1. Why did Corrie promise money to the stranger if she didn't trust him? What does her choice tell you about her character and values?
2. Why do you think Kapteyn was so angry when Corrie said Jesus' name?
3. Could Corrie or the Ten Booms have prevented the raid? If so, how?
4. Have you ever been in a situation where you didn't know whom you could trust? What was it like? Think about the way trust (or lack of trust) is portrayed in this book. Can you see a theme? What does *The Hiding Place* seem to say about the importance of being able to trust other people?

Chapter 10

Review Questions

1. Why didn't the chief interrogator in The Hague release Father, as he intended?
2. Why did Corrie apologize to her new cellmates in Scheveningen?
3. Why were the card games dangerous for Corrie?
4. What did the nurse at the hospital give Corrie?
5. What did *kalte kost* mean?
6. Who/what became Corrie's companion in solitary?
7. How did Corrie get news about her family? What was the news?

Thought Questions

1. Why do you think the Jewish man was unwilling to let go of his purse? Are there things you hold onto that tightly, even though they are relatively unimportant?
2. Why were the Germans so particular about where the prisoners walked?
3. Did it surprise you to learn that kind people like the nurse worked alongside German soldiers? Is it wrong to work for an evil system, even if it enables you to help people in ways you would not otherwise be able to?
4. What kind of victories do you think came from the Holocaust? Think carefully before you answer.

Chapter 11

Review Questions

1. Why did Corrie want to be taken to hut number 4 for her hearing?
2. What did Lieutenant Rahms call "a waste of time and energy"?
3. Why had Corrie been placed in solitary confinement?
4. What gift did Lieutenant Rahms give Corrie after her last hearing?
5. How did Corrie get to see and touch the members of her family?
6. How had the Jews escaped from the Beje?

Thought Questions

1. Why did Corrie describe herself as a professional? What kind of professional was she?
2. Which kind of interrogation would be harder to resist, a forceful one or a kind one? Why?
3. When the Lieutenant said he was in a prison, what kind of prison do you think he meant?
4. Why do you think God allows Christians to suffer? Would it be fair if only non-Christians suffered? Be prepared to explain your reasons.
5. How would you explain the existence of evil? Discuss this with your family.

Chapter 12

Review Questions

1. What was the last message Corrie received from the ants?
2. Where were Corrie and Betsie taken when they left Scheveningen?
3. What did the pink forms mean?
4. To what job was Corrie assigned? Why did Mr. Moorman scold Corrie for her work?
5. Who was Jan Vogel? How did Betsie change the way Corrie thought about him?
6. Why did Corrie look forward to September 1st?

7.   Why were the male prisoners executed?

Thought Questions
1.   Can you imagine Corrie and Betsie's disappointment when they realized they were not going to be freed? Would it be harder to return to prison life after a taste of freedom?
2.   How are people taught to hate? How are they taught to love? Are the two processes similar in any way? If so, how?
3.   Betsie said, "What better way could there be to spend our lives [than in prison camps]." Explain. Do you agree?
4.   Why didn't the officers want the prisoners to know that rations had been reduced on the front line?
5.   Do you think some sins are worse than others? What does the Bible say? Is it hard to believe that Hitler and Mother Teresa were equally sinners? Explain.

Chapter 13

Review Questions
1.   Where in Germany were Corrie and Betsie taken?
2.   Why did the women prisoners need to cut their hair?
3.   How did Corrie and Betsie get the vitamins and Bible past the guards?
4.   Why were the newcomers housed next to the punishment barracks?
5.   What was the Siemens Brigade?
6.   What was the miracle of the Davitamon bottle?
7.   Why did the guard whip Betsie?
8.   What changes had Betsie brought to Barracks 28?

Thought Questions
1.   Why didn't the adults in the German village look at the prisoners? Were they ashamed? Afraid? Discuss.
2.   Why do people describe the worst cruelty as one that is "detached"? What does "detached" mean?
3.   How could prisoners in a concentration camp be conquerors?
4.   What would it be like to have a number instead of a name? Is your name what defines you? Why or why not?
5.   If you attend church, do you go to a specific denomination? Would it be odd for you to worship with Baptists, Catholics, Presbyterians, Jews, or Apostolics? Why was it natural in prison? Do you agree with Corrie that "in darkness God's truth shines most clear"?

Chapter 14

Review Questions
1.   Why had Betsie been right to thank God for the fleas in the barracks?
2.   At the roll call, how did Corrie misunderstand the objects of Betsie's pity?
3.   How did Corrie escape being transferred to munitions work?
4.   What was the special temptation of concentration camp life?
5.   What did Corrie call her real sin?
6.   Describe Betsie's visions for the ministry after Ravensbruck.
7.   How had Betsie's face changed the last time Corrie saw her? What tied Corrie to Betsie afterward?

Thought Questions
1. Discuss the behavior of the nurses at the concentration camp. Was the way they cared for the patients marked for execution cruel or kind?
2. Have you ever wondered why God placed a trial in your life? Is it hard to wait for answers? What makes it possible to wait patiently?
3. Why is selfishness so easy to justify? Do you think Corrie was wrong for trying to protect Betsie? Are secret sins and blatant evil equal? What is the basis of your answer?
4. What do you think people will look like in Heaven? How might they be the same? Different?

Chapter 15

Review Questions
1. What prevented Corrie's immediate release after she was freed?
2. What was the most fatal disease of the concentration camp?
3. What did the guards give each prisoner before he left? What did prisoners have to sign?
4. What did Corrie mistake for a party at the hospital in Groningen?
5. Which of Corrie's family members were there to welcome her?
6. With whom did Corrie reunite on the trip to Haarlem?
7. How did Corrie realize that she could no longer work with the underground?
8. Where was the greatest hunger for Betsie's story?
9. What did the director of the relief organization propose to Corrie?
10. How were Betsie's last visions fulfilled?

Thought Questions
1. Why do you think the Nazis only released healthy prisoners?
2. Is evil the norm or the exception in our society?
3. What does the phrase, "there are no 'ifs' in God's kingdom" mean?
4. What would be the hardest part of adjusting to life after prison? What do you think Corrie was still waiting and looking for?
5. Can the evils of war ever truly be undone?
6. How do you think Betsie "knew" about Mrs. Bierens de Haan's house?
7. Why was it harder for the Dutch people to forgive fellow Dutchmen than Germans?
8. How could going back to a place of hurt (i.e., a concentration camp) result in healing? Why do you think God chose Corrie for this particular work?

Tanglewood Tales
Nathaniel Hawthorne

Introduction

Nathaniel Hawthorne (1804–1864) was born in Salem, Massachusetts and developed a love for reading and learning when he was kept in bed with a leg injury. Despite his love of knowledge, his uncle had to insist he attend college, after which Nathaniel published several short stories in magazines. Today he is known for the slightly dark and didactic tone of his stories, which often have religious themes. In 1853, he wrote *Tanglewood Tales*, a retelling of Greek myths, as a "sequel" to his *A Wonder-Book for Girls and Boys*. People loved *Tanglewood Tales*; mansions, neighborhoods, and an island have all been named after this collection of stories.

Reading Practice: Maps

Pick a character and draw his/her world or journey based on passages that describe places or talk about travel. Does the character cross any bodies of water? Ride a horse over a certain type of terrain? Enter a forest? See a mountain? Use all the setting clues and build the world as described.

When you're finished, look at a world map to see if any real cities or landmarks are mentioned in the story you chose. How is your map similar to the real map? How is it different? Why did you draw your map the way you did? Did anything in the story "steer you wrong"?

Going Deeper: Worldview

The ancient Greeks who originally invented these stories believed in Zeus, Hera, and Hades. They used stories to explain the world and glorify virtues such as loyalty, hospitality, and justice.

Nathaniel grew up in Puritan New England, surrounded by a solemn piety and uprightness. Later, Nathaniel met many transcendentalists: people who believed in embracing freedom and spirituality rather than getting too caught up in the physical world.

Where in *Tanglewood Tales* do you see Nathaniel keep to the ancient Greek values? Where do you see him suggest his own ideas about what's important? Does Nathaniel ever advocate for attention to the physical world, or maybe advocate against it?

The Minotaur

Review Questions

1. What test did Theseus have to perform in order to depart from his mother?
2. Where did Theseus want to go? Why?
3. Why did the city send men and maidens to the Minotaur? How long had this been a practice?
4. Who is Ariadne? Why did she want to help Theseus? How did she help?
5. What did Theseus promise his father before leaving? Did he fulfill his promise?

Thought Questions

1. What admirable qualities does Theseus exhibit?
2. What was Theseus' flaw?
3. What caused Theseus to forget to "hoist sunshiny sails"? Did King Aegeus act wisely?
4. How did you expect the story to end? What led you to think that way?

The Pygmies

Review Questions

1. Who were the Pygmies? Where were they from?
2. Who was the giant? What did he think about the Pygmies?
3. What was the one thing in the world that troubled the Pygmies? What did they do about it?
4. Who was the second giant? What was his quest?
5. What was Antaeus's secret to strength? How was he defeated?

Thought Questions

1. Did Antaeus deserve to be defeated? Why or why not?
2. What do you think is meant by "For these earth-born creatures are only difficult to conquer on their own ground, but may be easily managed if we can contrive to lift them into a loftier and purer region"? Can you apply that adage to other problems or situations? Is there a biblical principle that can be applied here? Read 1 Peter 5:7. What other verses might apply?
3. In *Walden*, Henry David Thoreau says, "…like pygmies we fight with cranes…" What is he meaning to say?
4. Who was more a faithful friend, Antaeus or the Pygmies? Why?

The Dragon's Teeth

Review Questions

1. Which brother was the first to give up hope of ever finding his sister? How did he feel when his companions said goodbye?
2. What happened to Thasus to cause him to give up the search for Europa? What preparations did he make in anticipation that one day Europa would show up at his palace?
3. Who advised Cadmus to seek out the Oracle of Delphi? Where was the Oracle of Delphi located? What question did Cadmus ask the oracle? Where did the oracle tell Cadmus he would find his home?
4. What did Cadmus do with the dragon's teeth? What happened almost immediately? What did the soldiers do?

5. Who helped Cadmus build the city? What was the name of the beautiful stranger who later appeared to Cadmus and lived with him there?

Thought Questions
1. Why do you think Europa's brothers, friend, and mother dedicated their lives to searching for her? Is there any cause to which you would unselfishly dedicate your life?
2. What Christian virtues does Cadmus display? Who are some people you know that display those same qualities? Would you consider them heroes? Why or why not?
3. Do you think King Agenor ever regretted his decision to banish his family from the palace until they brought back Europa? Do you think any of his sons or his wife ever regretted their decision to look for her forever? What makes you think so?

Circe's Palace

Review Questions
1. Why were King Ulysses and his men reluctant to explore the pleasant green island? What finally motivated them to decide to explore the island?
2. Why did the purple bird want so desperately to communicate with King Ulysses, and later Eurylochus? What was unique about the bird's appearance?
3. What curious thing did Eurylochus and his men see as they entered the palace? What did they hear?
4. What did Circe mean when she told the sailors to "assume their proper shapes"? Why were her victims turned into different types of animals?
5. How was King Ulysses able to outwit Circe? What did he compel her to do?

Thought Questions
1. King Picus went from being a proud king to a humble servant of his people, but it took being transformed temporarily into a flamboyant purple bird to effect the change in his heart. Do you think God has ever allowed you to go through a difficult situation for your own good or so you could help someone else later on?
2. If you were magically turned into an animal that represented your worst habit, what would you become?
3. Like the sailors who were single-mindedly focused on eating, when did your curiosity or determination to do something get you into trouble? What were the consequences?

The Pomegranate Seeds

Review Questions
1. What did Mother Ceres have care of? Who was her daughter? What was Proserpina's mistake?
2. What would keep Proserpina from ever going back home? What did King Pluto do about it?
3. Who helped Ceres find out what had happened to Proserpina? What happened to the crops while Ceres searched for King Pluto's kingdom?
4. What did Ceres do to Prince Demophoon? Why?
5. Proserpina did taste the pomegranate, but King Pluto did not know. Why did Proserpina tell the truth? What was the result?

Thought Questions

1. Was it fair for Mother Ceres to let the whole earth suffer with her? Why or why not?
2. Proserpina eventually felt something for King Pluto. Was it pity? Was it love? What was it?
3. Does Proserpina forgive King Pluto? Why? What does the Bible say about our enemies and forgiveness?
4. What is a lesson we can learn from this myth?
5. This myth may have been used by the ancient Greeks/Romans to explain the changing of the season. How is Proserpina's coming and going equated with the seasons?

The Golden Fleece

Review Questions

1. Who was Jason? Who and what was Chiron?
2. What was the one thing Jason wore of his father's? What happened to them?
3. Why did Jason go to King Pelias? What was the quest set before Jason?
4. What was the name given to the group of fifty brave adventurers that Jason assembled?
5. Which princess aided Jason in his quest? Why and how did she help?

Thought Questions

1. What is a *hero*?
2. Was Jason a hero or was he seeking the fleece for selfish reasons? Why?
3. What motivated the Argonauts to join Jason on the quest? Have you ever joined someone on a task or journey without knowing the end result?
4. What admirable qualities do Jason and the Argonauts exhibit?

Discussion Questions

1. Greek mythology has been passed down through the ages in written form, in artwork, and in other culture. Having various authors and many versions, the heroes' stories vary widely. Have you read or heard any of these myths previously? Were they exactly the same as they are told here? How are they the same? How are they different?

2. Tragic flaws (*hamartia*) are a literary device often used in Greek mythology. It is said tragic flaws were given to mortals by the gods. What were the flaws of the heroes in this book? Why do you think the writer of these myths gave them tragic flaws? What is the purpose?

3. As mentioned in the introduction, myths show the arrogance of humanity as the authors felt qualified to determine the origins of the world. How different is the perspective when we use God as our foundation? Why?

4. Read Acts 14:8–15. Paul and Barnabas and the apostles were teaching and performing miracles in Lystra (in modern-day Turkey). What did they call Paul and Barnabas after seeing the miracle? Why? What was the response of the apostles? What was the eventual response of the people (v. 19–20)?

5. Can knowing Greek mythology make us better Christians? Why or why not?

6. Do we have any modern-day mythology? Do we have any heroes today?

7. In each of these stories, the hero is on a quest for something. How do you think each of them would define "a good life"? What were they seeking? Do you think they ultimately found it? Why or why not? Do their priorities differ from your own definition of what makes a good life? What is the biblical definition of a good life? Explain.

A Gathering of Days
Joan W. Blos

Introduction

Joan Blos (1928–2017) has written picture books, a play, and several historical novels for children. She is best known for *A Gathering of Days*, which was written in 1979, and won the Newbery Medal in 1980. This fictional journal of a girl growing up in New England in the 1830s deals with questions of ethics, friendship, and learning to deal with the hardships of daily life.

Reading Practice: Chronologies

Because it is written as a journal, *A Gathering of Days* is already laid out in chronological order. However, since journals keep track of everything from life-changing events to small everyday occurrences, a timeline will help you keep track of the big events in Catherine's life. For this book, focus on the relationships between events. As you create your timeline, draw arrows from earlier events to the later events they influence.

Remember, although it is written as a journal, *A Gathering of Days* is actually fiction. Try to identify any repeating patterns in the events on your timeline, and think about how Blos uses this form (the journal) to tell a story. When you finish the book, take a minute to imagine how the timeline, and the story, might have to change if it were written in a more traditional form.

Going Deeper: Worldview

A Gathering of Days presents the world as it appears to Catherine Hall, a thirteen-year-old girl living in New Hampshire in 1830. Although you may find you have some things in common with Catherine, some parts of her experience will be different from your own. As a character, Catherine does not stop to explain or question everything about her world. As you read, ask questions about Catherine's worldview. What does she assume about religion? About people who are different from her? About family responsibilities? About friendship?

Catherine's worldview within the book is one layer, but another level is the worldview of the novel itself, which was written in the twentieth century. Think about the choices Blos requires Catherine to make and the situations she confronts. Finally, ask yourself what features of life in the 1830s *A Gathering of Days* might be encouraging you to challenge or question.

Chapter 1

Review Questions
1. To whom was this journal given? On what occasion?
2. How old was Catherine when she began writing in her journal?
3. What lesson did Father illustrate with the story about the headless woman?
4. On November 4, 1830, what frightened Catherine on the way home from school?
5. Whom did Mrs. Shipman want Father to meet, and why?
6. What did Father say should be done with runaway bound boys?

Thought Questions
1. Why do people write in journals?
2. How would you describe Catherine's daily life? What does she see as her role in the family? How are her expectations and desires different from yours?
3. Father said intelligence was given to us so we could "distinguish right from wrong, and knowing right, may do so." What do you think is the proper use of intelligence?

Chapter 2

Review Questions
1. Why was Sophy going to be sent to Lowell at age fifteen?
2. "Why are a scolding woman's hands and a fur cap alike?"
3. For what offense was Joshua Nelson thrashed?
4. What did Mrs. Shipman's sister bring that excited Catherine and Cassie?
5. How did the family celebrate Thanksgiving? What was Catherine's wish?

Thought Questions
1. What does "To thine own self be true" mean? Do you think it is a good proverb?
2. What does Thanksgiving mean to you? Why do families celebrate Thanksgiving together?
3. What does Catherine's description of Thanksgiving tell you about her family's values?

Chapter 3

Review Questions
1. What did Catherine lose (November 29, 1830)?
2. Why did Aunt Lucy come to visit the Halls?
3. Where did Catherine find her book? What was written in it?
4. How did Catherine care for Matty's cough?
5. What did Asa show Catherine in the woods?

Thought Questions
1. Asa said, "Who are we to judge [the man who asked for help]?" Do you agree? Explain.
2. What do you learn about Asa's and Catherine's characters by the way they react to the request of the "phantom"?

Chapter 4

Review Questions
1. Who was accused of stealing the Shipmans' pies? Why was he/she accused?
2. Why was Cassie angry with Catherine (December 14, 1830)?

3. For what offense was Cassie punished at school?
4. What was Cassie and Catherine's answer to the phantom's appeal?
5. Why was Catherine afraid the phantom had been discovered?

Thought Questions
1. Do you think the phantom was "sinned against" or a "dangerous sinner"? What basis did you use for your judgment?
2. What proverbs did Cassie and Catherine relate to their situation? Are the two mutually exclusive? Do you think proverbs oversimplify ethical questions?
3. What do you think is the highest virtue? Why?
4. What does the color red mean to you? Why did Catherine use that color in her message?

Chapter 5

Review Questions
1. What note did Father leave for Catherine on December 24? What did it mean?
2. Describe Catherine's Christmas.
3. What was the second phantom that Catherine saw?
4. Who made dinner on New Year's Day?

Thought Questions
1. How was Catherine's Christmas different from yours? Would you call hers a happy Christmas? What does her celebration of Christmas tell you about her community?
2. Asa preferred to take a beating than risk another's life by his denial. What does that tell you about his character?

Chapter 6

Review Questions
1. Why didn't Cassie and Catherine have to take Arithmetic?
2. What lines did Asa, Cassie, and Catherine choose for penmanship practice?
3. Why did Catherine call January 13 "*half* a holiday"?
4. What was the "breaking out"? To which holiday did Catherine compare it?
5. Who came to visit after the breaking out?

Thought Questions
1. Does it seem fair to you that girls didn't study math? What was the reason? Do you agree? Did Catherine question this assumption? If not, why not?
2. What does your family do differently when you have guests? Why? What does this say about your culture's views on hospitality?

Chapter 7

Review Questions
1. According to Catherine, what determined how oppressive a disability would be?
2. What had Father promised to Catherine's baby brother, Nathaniel?
3. What had happened to Nathaniel?
4. What was the motto of *The Liberator*?
5. What was Catherine too shy to tell Asa?
6. Of what was Teacher Holt accused? How did he answer the accusations?

Thought Questions
1. What do you think of Father's idea (See February 22, 1831) about resettling former slaves in Africa? Discuss the pros and cons of that argument. Do you agree with Uncle Jack instead?
2. Why do you think Father was opposed to having a black neighbor? Was Father a racist? What does the term "racist" mean, in your opinion?
3. Should teachers be allowed to teach morals in school? Try to think about both sides of the argument before you answer.
4. Do you agree with Teacher Holt that "in a nation founded in Freedom, the Liberty of every man ought to be tested, assessed, & debated in every age, and decade, of that nation's life"? If so, does that change the way you answer the previous question? Why or why not? How would you test the liberty of every man?

Chapter 8

Review Questions
1. Why did Cassie's mother say every winter should have a dispute?
2. How was the matter of Teacher Holt's lodging resolved?
3. How did Teacher Holt get around his pledge to the district?
4. Why was March 18, 1831 a special day?
5. Why did New Englanders start the Sabbath by the almanac and end it by the sunset?

Thought Questions
1. How would you answer Catherine's question (March 11) about discipline?
2. Do you think Teacher Holt's method of evading his pledge was the right thing to do? Was it respectful of the townspeople's authority?

Chapter 9

Review Questions
1. What happened to Joshua Nelson's mother?
2. Who was the stranger who was looking for Merchant Preston? Why had he come back?
3. What did Joshua see at the sugaring off?
4. What prank did Matty and Catherine play on April Fools' Day?

Thought Questions
1. Is it possible to go back and reclaim childhood? Why or why not?
2. Is it important to repay debts, even if they have been forgotten? Do you think debts ever expire in terms of moral obligation? If so, when?

Chapter 10

Review Questions
1. What did Asa want to give Sophy?
2. Who gave Catherine the flowers (April 13, 1831)?
3. Why did the girls have to spend April 14 inside sewing?
4. What did Father take with him to Boston? What was his news when he came back?
5. When was the wedding to be held? Why did Catherine find this odd?

Thought Questions
1. What does *ab[e]cedarian* mean? Where does the word comes from?
2. Why do you think people traveled so rarely in Catherine's time? Name three factors.
3. What can you tell about Ann Higham based on the letter she sent Catherine?
4. How do "Joy and sorrow [...] each makes [their] own season"? Explain.

Chapter 11

Review Questions
1. Why did the Jew price some scissors higher than others?
2. Why did Father buy a new jacket and take a second load of goods for his trip to Boston?
3. Describe Mistress Higham and Daniel.
4. When the Shipmans visited, who finally put the company at ease?

Thought Questions
1. Do you think Catherine did not invite the Jewish peddler into the house because he was a Jew or because he was a peddler? Discuss.
2. What does it mean to call someone "mother"? Why was Catherine unwilling to do so?
3. What do you think it was like for Mistress Higham to be compared to Father's first wife?

Chapter 12

Review Questions
1. Why was Mistress Higham offended by Uncle Jack's story? What was Father's reaction?
2. What was the picture in the mural at Cassie's house? How did the stenciller achieve the appearance of distance?
3. What was different about Summer School? Why didn't all of the students attend?
4. Why did Catherine tell Mistress Higham about the "phantom"?

Thought Questions
1. Mistress Higham said, "Let me remember this thankful moment later, when I've doubts." Explain.
2. How does prayer bring people together? What effect did it have on Catherine's family?
3. What does Mistress Higham's response to the story of the phantom tell you about her character?
4. Do you think Catherine's punishment was fair? Discuss. Why do you think Catherine cried when Mistress Higham offered to help her make the replacement quilt?

Chapter 13

Review Questions
1. Why did Catherine choose the Mariner's compass quilt pattern?
2. Why were Catherine and the others surprised to meet Joshua Nelson at school?
3. What was the moral of the quilt-making process?
4. What made the orator's speech funny?
5. What name did Daniel suggest Matty and Catherine call their stepmother?

Thought Questions
1. Why did Daniel want to know if the story about the horse was true? Is it important to know the difference between a story and a true story? Are both equally valuable?
2. Would it be hard to go from being in charge of a household to being under someone else's control? How would your way of thinking have to change?
3. How did Catherine's community celebrate July 4? What does this tell you about their priorities? Their values?
4. Catherine said, "A soldier's prayer is even more forceful than one by a minister." Explain. Do you agree with her reasoning?

Chapter 14

Review Questions
1. Who was getting married?
2. Why was Sophy tired of Aunt Lucy's happiness?
3. Why was Mammann concerned when Daniel and Asa went fishing?
4. How did Cassie get sick?
5. Why did Mammann write to Boston?
6. What happened on August 20, 1831?

Thought Questions
1. How would you interpret Father's story about the butter? Do you think he believed in witchcraft? What lesson do you think he intended the story to make?

Chapter 15

Review Questions
1. Why did Aunt Lucy dye all of her dresses?
2. How did Mammann handle her grief? How did Mrs. Shipman?
3. What was the Wiley slide?
4. What had Catherine forgotten about Daniel?

Thought Questions
1. Why do people wear black to funerals? Why do you think Catherine and the girls wore white to Cassie's funeral?
2. What are some different ways people deal with grief? Compare the responses here to the methods used in *Where the Red Fern Grows*. Why do you think they are so different?
3. If you knew a friend was near death, what would you want to tell them?
4. Do you see the hand of God in storms? Are they under His control? Do they serve His purposes?

Chapter 16

Review Questions
1. When was the first time Catherine laughed after Cassie's death? What made her laugh?
2. What news came on September 13, 1831?
3. What were the main arguments for and against freeing the slaves?
4. Why did Daniel look forward to the start of school?
5. For what did Mammann discipline Matty?

Thought Questions

1. Is it harmful to cling to memories about loved ones who have died? Why or why not?
2. Catherine said, "Strange, that one speaks of these deaths and slayings and is not disposed to tears." Why not, in your opinion? Why do people cry?
3. What does the quote, "We mourn all deaths with each particular grief" mean?
4. Why was Mammann offended when the slave rebellion was compared to the War of Independence? Do you think that was a fair comparison? Why or why not?

Chapter 17

Review Questions

1. What did Sophy pin to her bodice when she left?
2. Who sent Catherine the two pieces of lace? Why did the message make Catherine cry?
3. Why did Uncle Jack visit less often after Mammann came?
4. Was Catherine pleased when Father gave the Barlow knife to Daniel?
5. What happened when the new teacher tried to whip Joshua Nelson?

Thought Questions

1. What makes moving exciting for some people and frightening for others?
2. Why do you think Father gave the Barlow knife to Daniel instead of Catherine? What does this suggest about the way their society viewed sons and daughters?
3. What is the prose of your life? The poetry?

Chapter 18

Review Questions

1. Why were Matty and Catherine withdrawn from school?
2. What made the first day of homeschooling funny to Catherine?
3. What did Catherine do with the phantom's lace?
4. What did the letter from Aunt Lucy ask Catherine to do? What was her response?
5. When was the concluding letter written? What was the context?
6. To whom was Catherine's journal later given?

Thought Questions

1. What does Mammann's faith in books tell you about her character?
2. Do you think Father changed his mind about Catherine's helping the phantom? Explain. Why did Catherine compare Cassie to the phantom? Do you think that meant she had changed the way she thought about the stranger?
3. Is obedience defined by trust or by submission? What is the difference?
4. What did Catherine learn in the course of her "gathering of days"? What did she learn to accept?

Where the Red Fern Grows
Wilson Rawls

Introduction

Wilson Rawls (1913–1984) began to write stories while traveling in North and South America, but because he had been forced to drop out of school at a young age, he struggled with grammar and the mechanics of writing. His first novel, *Where the Red Fern Grows*, is a semi-autobiographical story that Rawls reportedly destroyed because he was embarrassed by his poor English. He later rewrote it, and it was published in book form in 1961. Although *Where the Red Fern Grows* was originally marketed as an adult novel, its themes of hard work, friendship, and loss have made it a popular children's book as well.

Reading Practice: Glossary of Terms

Glossaries do not have to be verbal only—they can also be visual. Although the vocabulary of *Where the Red Fern Grows* is not difficult in general, the book is set in the Ozark Mountains of northeastern Oklahoma, and some of the slang and local terms may be unfamiliar to you. In addition, unless you live in the Ozarks, you may not have a mental picture of some of the wildlife and scenery Rawls describes.

If you come across an unfamiliar word, take a minute to write it down, along with a brief definition. If the book refers to an animal, plant, or tree you have never seen, try to find an image so you can picture what it looks like. Keep your glossary beside you for quick reference as you read.

Going Deeper: Character Development

The subtitle of *Where the Red Fern Grows* is "The Story of Two Dogs and a Boy." Although the two dogs do not speak and are clearly not human, Billy's character is formed by his experiences as a dog owner. As you read, pay attention to the interactions between Billy and his dogs, and think about how Billy grows as a result of each adventure. Also consider the way Billy's relationship with his dogs affects his relationships with the people in his life.

Chapter 1

Review Questions
1. What did the narrator hear on his way home?
2. Why did the narrator decide to help the old hound?
3. How did the narrator know the dog was traveling a long distance?
4. What were the marks of a hunting dog?
5. In which objects did the narrator see the story he was about to tell?

Thought Questions
1. Have you ever had a special pet? Why do you think humans and animals bond so closely with each other?
2. Is it reasonable to attribute human emotions to animals?
3. Do you think the narrator did the right thing in sending the dog on its way? Why or why not?

Chapter 2

Review Questions
1. What kind of dogs did Billy want?
2. Which were Billy's favorite animal tracks?
3. What did Papa buy for Billy at the store?
4. What was the first thing Billy trapped?
5. What happened when hunting season opened?

Thought Questions
1. Have you ever experienced the kind of puppy love Billy described? Do you think boys are affected more than girls are?
2. Have you ever wanted something you couldn't have? How did you handle the situation? Is causing trouble a good way to get what you want? Why or why not?
3. Are all powerful desires a good thing? A bad thing? What is the purpose of having unfulfilled longings? Discuss.

Chapter 3

Review Questions
1. Why did Billy visit the place where the fishermen had been camping?
2. How much did puppies cost? How did Billy plan to buy them?
3. How long did it take Billy to earn the money?

Thought Questions
1. What Bible verse did Billy think of when he was praying for dogs? Do you think he took the verse out of context?
2. What is the most money you have ever saved? Could you be as patient as Billy was? What does his determination to buy the dogs tell you about his character? Compare Billy's perseverance to Nat's in *Carry On, Mr. Bowditch*. How are they similar? How are they different?
3. Why do you think Grandpa cried when Billy showed him the money?

Chapter 4

Review Questions
1. How did Billy get to Tahlequah?
2. How far away was the town? What two landmarks guided Billy on his journey?
3. Why was Billy afraid of the marshal?
4. What did Billy buy at the store?
5. What did Billy mistake for a party?
6. Why did the other boy call Billy a hillbilly?

Thought Questions
1. Why was Billy afraid to tell his father about the dogs?

2. Why do you think the two women described Billy as "wild"? What did they mean by the word? Was it a fair description?
3. Why do children call each other names? What is the difference between giving people nicknames and calling them names?
4. Are "town people" and "country people" very different today?

Chapter 5

Review Questions
1. How did the townspeople react when they saw Billy with his pups?
2. Who stopped the fight? What did he think of the boys who had been fighting?
3. What happened during the night? How did Billy respond? What did his dogs do?

Thought Questions
1. How do you think Billy felt when he saw his puppies for the first time?
2. Do you think Billy made the right decision to fight the town boys?
3. How did Billy characterize his puppies? What did he emphasize most? Can you tell what he valued by these descriptions?
4. Billy said he was ready to die for his dogs. Why do you think he valued them so highly?

Chapter 6

Review Questions
1. What did Billy name his dogs?
2. How did Billy's parents react when he got home?
3. What reasons did Billy give for his dislike of the town?

Thought Questions
1. Think of a time in your life when a situation came together like a puzzle. Could you see all the pieces along the way? When did you finally see how it all fit together?
2. Why was Mama upset to hear that Billy didn't like the town?
3. Papa said, "There's more to an education than just reading and writing." Do you agree? What else is there?
4. Did God answer Billy's prayer for puppies? Think carefully before you answer.

Chapter 7

Review Questions
1. What obstacle stood in the way of Billy's hunting?
2. Explain Grandpa's trap. Why did it work?
3. Why did Papa say the traps were not sportsmanlike?
4. What was the hardest part of training the pups?

Thought Questions
1. Do people ever behave like coons (unwilling to let a small thing go in exchange for freedom)?
2. Read Luke 18:18–25. How does this story compare to the coon's actions?
3. Why do you think parents get angry when they are scared? How are fear and anger related?
4. What does it mean to be a good sportsman? Why is it important to be sportsman-like if you hunt?

Chapter 8

Review Questions

1. Why did Papa say Mama was worried about Billy's hunting?
2. How, according to Billy's sister, did the dogs know they were going hunting?
3. How did the coon fool the dogs?
4. Why was Billy dismayed when he reached the treed coon? Why couldn't he leave the coon in the tree?
5. What did Papa tell Billy to do? How did Billy convince Papa to let him stay?

Thought Questions

1. Papa said women worry more than men. Do you agree? If so, why might that be true?
2. Do you think Mama wanted to keep Billy a little boy forever? Why or why not?
3. Should Billy have given up when the coon ran up the big sycamore? Why or why not?
4. Are promises important even if they are made to animals or to yourself? Explain.

Chapter 9

Review Questions

1. What trick did Grandpa devise to allow Billy to sleep?
2. Where was Old Dan the next morning?
3. Why was Billy disappointed with Little Ann? How was he proven wrong?
4. What made the tree fall?

Thought Questions

1. Is it ever okay to give up? Can you think of a situation where giving up would be right?
2. Why did Grandpa think every boy should have to cut down a big tree? What does a task like that do for your character?
3. Have you ever made a judgment before you knew the whole story?
4. Do you think God answered Billy's prayer? Explain. Based on what you have read so far, how do you think Billy would characterize God?

Chapter 10

Review Questions

1. What did Billy do with the money he earned from his coonskins?
2. What did Billy notice Grandpa doing when he counted Billy's furs?
3. How did Grandpa react when Billy exaggerated too much?
4. What happened in "The Cyclone Timber"?

Thought Questions

1. Does it seem odd that Billy gave his money to his father? If so, why?
2. Is it lying to stretch the truth? Defend your answer. If your answer was no, how would you define lying? If your answer was yes, do you think it is wrong to lie in jest? In defense of someone else?

Chapter 11

Review Questions

1. Why was Old Dan working the trail slowly when they went out after the storm?

2. What happened to Little Ann? What did Billy use to save her?
3. Why didn't Billy tell his parents what had happened?

Thought Questions
1. Have you ever felt totally helpless? What did you think about? What did you do?
2. Billy said his prayer "wasn't said with just words"? What do you think he meant? Have you ever said a prayer like that? When?
3. Mama told Billy that God only answers prayers said from the heart. What did she mean? Do you agree?

Chapter 12

Review Questions
1. Whom did Billy meet at Grandpa's store? Why didn't he like them?
2. What did Rainie say about Grandpa?
3. What did Rainie and Rubin want to bet Billy?

Thought Questions
1. What makes someone mean? Is anyone "born mean"?
2. Was Grandpa wise to urge Billy to accept the Pritchards' bet? What does this encounter tell you about his character?
3. Was it wrong for Billy to accept the bet? Did he do it for the right reasons? If you do something wrong, but you have good motives for doing it, is it still wrong?
4. What is the best way to respond when someone is taunting you?

Chapter 13

Review Questions
1. What was the ghost coon's trick?
2. How did Rubin twist the terms of the bet?
3. How did Rubin die?
4. What did Billy take to the Pritchards' graveyard?

Thought Questions
1. How could Billy have avoided the situation with the Pritchards? Where did he go wrong? Was he responsible for Rubin's death? If not, who was?
2. Is there value in portraying violence realistically? Is violence in books different than violence in movies? How would you decide when a book or movie is too violent?
3. Why did Billy think of his mother when Rubin died?
4. Why didn't the Pritchards cry? Does that mean they didn't care? Why or why not?

Chapter 14

Review Questions
1. What did Grandpa want to show Billy?
2. How did Grandpa know Billy's dogs were good enough to be in the championship?
3. What did Billy's youngest sister ask from him?
4. What did Billy tell Papa was strange about Little Ann?

Thought Questions
1. Was it Grandpa's fault that Rubin died? Was his suggestion that Billy forget the incident good advice? Why or why not?

2. Why are some things impossible to forget?
3. When was the last time you noticed the "God-sent gifts" around you? What keeps you from appreciating the beauty around you? Would you describe God as an artist?
4. Why did Billy feel strange when he saw his ax? Were his fears rational? What does his eventual response tell you about his character?

Chapter 15

Review Questions
1. What did Billy hear during the night? Why was he concerned?
2. What made the other hounds different than Little Ann and Old Dan?
3. Which dog did Billy enter in the contest for best-looking hound? What were the results?
4. What number of coons did Billy have to beat in order to win?

Thought Questions
1. Why do hounds hunt in pairs? Can you learn something from that characteristic?
2. What are some local superstitions you have heard? Would a man go crazy if he believed them all? What causes superstitions? Do they have any basis in truth?

Chapter 16

Review Questions
1. How did Grandpa get wet on the hunt?
2. How many coons did Little Ann and Old Dan catch the first night of eliminations?
3. How many pairs of hounds were in the championship?
4. What did Old Dan and Little Ann do for each other after they killed the first coon?

Thought Questions
1. Who were the most important characters in the hunt, Billy and Grandpa, or Little Ann and Old Dan? What made them a team?
2. How do you think Little Ann and Old Dan knew the hunt was important? Can humans and animals communicate? If so, how?

Chapter 17

Review Questions
1. What kind of storm began during the championship round?
2. Why wouldn't the dogs come in, according to Billy?
3. What happened to Grandpa?
4. How many coons came out of the hollow tree?
5. Why did Little Ann and Old Dan run off again?
6. What did Billy do with the coon skins?

Thought Questions
1. Why did Billy refuse to leave his dogs? Was it fair for him to put the other men at risk by staying? Do you think he valued the dogs more than the people with him?
2. Why did Grandpa tell Billy to act like a coon hunter? What did he mean? Do you think a coon hunter is a good thing to aspire to be?

Chapter 18

Review Questions
1. How did the hunters know to look for Billy and the other men?
2. Why did Mr. Kyle hope Billy's dogs had the coon treed?
3. What had happened to the dogs? How did the men save them?
4. What did Billy win? What did he do with his prize?
5. What did Mama do when Papa gave her the money? What did Billy overhear Mama and Papa discussing?

Thought Questions
1. How did the hunters help one another? Do sportsmen today behave this way? Explain.
2. Are animals capable of feeling love? What is the difference between loyalty and love? Is one better? Which one?
3. Do humans show the kind of love Little Ann and Old Dan showed?

Chapter 19

Review Questions
1. What did the dogs tree in the Cyclone Timber?
2. What happened when the animal sprang at Billy?
3. How did Old Dan die? Where did Billy bury him?
4. What happened to Little Ann after Old Dan died?
5. Where did Little Ann go when she disappeared? How did she die?
6. How had the dogs answered Mama's prayers?
7. Why did Papa think God had taken away the dogs?

Thought Questions
1. Why do you think the dogs saved Billy from the mountain lion?
2. What does the phrase, "there is a little good in all evil" mean? Do you agree?
3. Why do you think God let Old Dan die?
4. Can people die because they lose the will to live? How does that kill someone?
5. Had Billy done anything wrong to cause his dogs to die? Explain.
6. Discuss Papa's and Mama's responses to Billy's grief. Do you agree with their ideas about God, heaven, and prayer?

Chapter 20

Review Questions
1. What grew over the graves of Billy's dogs?
2. What old Indian legend did Billy remember?
3. Did Billy ever go back to the Ozarks?

Thought Questions
1. Do you think there was truth in the old legend? If not, why did people believe it?
2. Why did Billy say part of his life was buried in the Ozarks? Explain.
3. How did Billy's character change as a result of Little Ann and Old Dan?
4. Billy said he wanted to go back to the Ozarks, God willing. Do you think Billy's experiences with Little Ann and Old Dan changed his beliefs about God? If so, how?

Crispin: The Cross of Lead
Avi

Introduction

Avi (1937–) achieved success as a writer only after struggling to make it through school with a learning disability (dyslexia). After becoming a successful writer, Avi continued to return to schools, encouraging other children with learning disabilities. *Crispin: The Cross of Lead* was published in 2002, and it won the 2003 Newbery Award. Set in the 14th century, *Crispin* explores a young boy's quest to discover his identity and the nature of freedom.

Reading Practice: Chronologies

A timeline allows you to visualize the events of a book in chronological order. For *Crispin*, which takes place over days, not years, try to focus on the places where events are narrated at a rapid pace and where the narration slows down to include conversations or lengthy description.

As you read, create a timeline for the major events and turning points in Crispin's adventures. Since this is historical fiction, find a timeline of actual events in England in 1377 and the surrounding years, and think about the connections between the historical events and the events in the novel. (Also see the "Historical Note" in the back of most editions of the book.)

Going Deeper: Imagery

Although England may be a familiar name to you, this book takes place hundreds of years ago. In order to make the story approachable, Avi had to use words to create a setting that would seem real to readers.

When you read a particularly vivid passage in this book (see Chapters 4 and 16 for examples), take a minute to sketch the scene. Pay special attention to visual adjectives like color and texture. Think about ways to represent sounds and smells. Imagine you are responsible for bringing the book to life in a work of art. As you read, take note of similarities and differences between this fourteenth-century setting and the setting of *The Door in the Wall*.

Chapter 1

Review Questions
1. With what event does the book open?
2. Why did they place the woman with her feet toward the east?
3. Who was John Aycliffe? Why did the boy fear him?

Thought Questions
1. Have you ever been ashamed of something outside your control? Can you explain the feeling? What is the root of shame?
2. Why were prayers spoken in Latin if most people did not understand Latin?
3. In the boy's situation, do you think you would have said of God, "His will be done"? What does this reveal to you about the boy's understanding of God?

Chapter 2

Review Questions
1. Where did the boy awake?
2. What happened when John Aycliffe spotted the boy?
3. For what acts did the boy believe God was punishing him?

Thought Questions
1. How would you characterize this society based on the first few chapters? What do they value? What do they believe about God? How is their community organized?
2. Do you associate darkness with evil? Is there any truth to such beliefs? Discuss.
3. Why do you think people swore by things like "the bowels of Christ"? Are such oaths different from curse words today? If so, how?
4. Are misfortunes punishments from God? Think carefully before you answer.

Chapter 3

Review Questions
1. How had the boy's father died?
2. What was the boy's name?
3. What was a *serf*?
4. How often did Asta's son see Lord Furnival?
5. What two events, according to Asta's son, gave distinction to life?

Thought Questions
1. What did it mean for families to live in the light of a father's name and rank? What did it mean for daughters? For widows? For orphans?
2. Do you agree with the description of serfs as neither slaves nor free people? Do you think people can be satisfied with partial freedom?
3. Describe the worldview of Asta's son. With what points would you disagree?

Chapter 4

Review Questions
1. What was the name for the early morning prayers?
2. What was a *cottar*?
3. What did the bailiff and the reeve do to Asta's cottage?
4. What two things did the villagers gain from their obedience to the steward?

Thought Questions
1. Do you think set times for prayer are a good idea? Give an argument for each side.
2. According to Asta's son, "The steward said we belonged to our lord." How is this condition different than slavery?

Chapter 5

Review Questions
1. How did Asta's son know something important was happening in the village?
2. What three men spoke to the crowd outside the church?

Thought Questions
1. The church was the center of Asta's son's village. What is the center of your town or city? Why do you think churches are no longer the center of most cities?

Chapter 6

Review Questions
1. Who was the one person Asta's son trusted?
2. What kept him from approaching the village?

Thought Questions
1. If they were serfs as well, why do you think the men of the village cooperated with the steward to hunt a fellow serf?

Chapter 7

Review Questions
1. Asta's son heard Matthew and Luke say he had been accused of what crime?
2. How had the steward responded to complaints from the villagers?
3. What were *Vespers* and *Compline*?

Thought Questions
1. Did the steward have absolute power? Was he physically stronger than all of the villagers put together? How did he control them?
2. How can a group of people without free speech or legal rights bring about change?

Chapter 8

Review Questions
1. Who was the stranger that Aycliffe had met in the woods? What news had he brought?
2. What did it mean that Asta's son had been declared a "wolf's head"?
3. What was Asta's son's real name?
4. What did Father Quinel say were his options for escape?
5. What did Father Quinel reveal about his mother? About the lead cross he wore?

Thought Questions
1. What did it mean to claim sanctuary? Do you agree with this practice? Why or why not?
2. Can someone become non-human because another person says so? What makes someone human?
3. Can men and women know the will of God? Should they try?
4. Is the ability to read and write still a symbol of status? Explain.

Chapter 9

Review Questions
1. Whom did Crispin meet on his way to the church? What was the newcomer's message?
2. What was the reward on Crispin's head?
3. What did Goodwife Peregrine give Crispin?

Thought Questions
1. Are names powerful? Can a change of name make you a different person? Think about the biblical examples of Sarah, Abraham, and Jacob. Does this change your answer?

Chapter 10

Review Questions
1. Why did Cerdic want Crispin to go west?
2. When and why did Cerdic leave Crispin's side?

Thought Questions
1. Why do you think boundaries and borders were marked by crosses? Does it cheapen the significance of the cross to use it in so many different ways?

Chapter 11

Review Questions
1. How did Crispin escape the trap?
2. What did Crispin find near the southern boundary cross?

Thought Questions
1. Why did Crispin believe God had abandoned him? If you were there, how would you respond to his statement?

Chapter 12

Review Questions
1. What did Crispin see in his future?
2. Why did he think he would go to hell if he died alone?

Thought Questions
1. How are Crispin's beliefs similar to and different from your own?
2. Was Crispin to blame for Father Quinel's death? If not, who was?
3. How does Avi portray Christianity in this novel? Is it a positive picture? Neutral? Negative? Discuss.

Chapter 13

Review Questions
1. What noise awakened Crispin?
2. What was in Goodwife Peregrine's pouch?
3. What did Crispin remember after he saw the bailiff?

Thought Questions

1. If you had never had to make decisions before, would it be difficult to begin? Does the same thing apply to freedom? To independence? Compare and contrast the ideas here with what you read in *Amos Fortune, Free Man*.
2. Is decision-making hard for you? If so, what do you do to avoid making decisions? Is it easier to act or to make a decision?

Chapter 14

Review Questions

1. What did Crispin see on the road through the mist? How did he interpret it?
2. How did his perspective change as a result?
3. Which path did he choose, and why?

Thought Questions

1. Why do you think Crispin reacted the way he did to the sight of the dead man?
2. Why do you think the sight of death produced a desire to live? If death frightened Crispin, why did he follow the path that reminded him of the dead man's eye?

Chapter 15

Review Questions

1. Why did the village Crispin found look so unusual?
2. How did he explain the village's appearance?
3. What did Crispin hear as he passed the church?

Thought Questions

1. Are plagues and natural disasters punishments from God? Why or why not?
2. Why do you think God allows all things to "wear and waste away"?

Chapter 16

Review Questions

1. Describe the man Crispin found in the church.
2. What was Crispin's excuse for traveling alone?
3. For what reason did Crispin accuse the big man of treason? How did the man react?
4. What did the man do when Crispin reached for the bread?

Thought Questions

1. What is the difference between "It is as it is" and "Let it be as it may be"?
2. What does *treason* mean to you? Do you think the man was speaking treasonously?

Chapter 17

Review Questions

1. What did the stranger want to know from Crispin?
2. What did he do when he released Crispin?

Thought Questions

1. Why do you think the stranger seized Crispin? Did he want to help him or use him?

2. The stranger said, "Save yourself? […] No man can do so on his own." What do you think he meant? Do you agree?

Chapter 18

Review Questions
1. What did the big man tell Crispin would happen to him now?
2. What did he make Crispin swear?

Thought Questions
1. Do you consider it theft to hold back wool with the purpose of feeding a sick child? How would you define *theft*?
2. Have you ever taken an oath? Broken one? Did you take it as seriously as Crispin did?

Chapter 19

Review Questions
1. What unusual question did the big man ask Crispin about the future?
2. Whom did the man advise Crispin to trust?
3. What was the man's trade? What was his name?

Thought Questions
1. Do you think men are made to live without masters?
2. Explain: "The only one who can betray you is yourself." Do you agree with the stranger?
3. What do the stranger's comments about freedom suggest about his character? Was it inconsistent for him to force Crispin to serve him? Discuss.
4. The man said his task was to stay alive and measure the kingdom with his feet, eyes, and ears. What does that mean? How could you measure the world in that way?

Chapter 20

Review Questions
1. Why didn't Crispin run away from Bear?
2. Why were there no people around as they walked?

Thought Questions
1. Why didn't Bear want Crispin to call him "Sir"? Does this seem strange to you, if he wanted to be treated as Crispin's master? Was he a different kind of master?

Chapter 21

Review Questions
1. For what career had Bear originally been destined? What changed his plans?
2. How did his early training protect him?
3. Why did Bear need Crispin?

Thought Questions
1. What makes someone a priest or minister?
2. Had God abandoned Bear? Have you ever confused human failings with God's failings? Discuss.

Chapter 22

Review Questions
1. Why did Bear tie Crispin to a tree?
2. What kind of stories did Bear tell Crispin by the fire that night?
3. How did Bear describe Lord Furnival?

Thought Questions
1. Is it possible to trust someone immediately?
2. How does war especially test Christians? Is it possible to fight a war in a Christian manner? What would that look like?

Chapter 23

Review Questions
1. Why, according to Crispin, was his mother silent? How did his mother treat him?
2. How had Bear escaped the Great Death?

Thought Questions
1. Is it possible to love and despise someone at the same time? What might cause that combination of emotions? Are love and hate related in any way?

Chapter 24

Review Questions
1. What advice did Bear give Crispin?
2. Why did Bear say the cross was useless?
3. Which two of Bear's teachings did Crispin find hard to reconcile?

Thought Questions
1. Bear said, "The greater a man's—or boy's—ignorance of the world, the more certain he is that he sits in the center of that world." Explain. Do you agree?
2. In your opinion, is anyone only good or only bad?
3. Do you agree with Bear's theology? Explain your answer.
4. Has God given every man a position in life, or do we make our own destiny?
5. What does it mean to live by questions? If you lived by questions, what questions would you ask?

Chapter 25

Review Questions
1. What was Crispin afraid would happen if he disappointed Bear?
2. What did Bear make Crispin do at the river? Why?
3. Why didn't Bear think Crispin would be recognized in the villages?
4. How did Bear propose to make Crispin matter?

Thought Questions
1. Is it hypocritical to think one thing and do another? Why or why not?
2. Is there a balance between being content with the way you were made and trying to improve yourself?
3. What lesson do you think Bear was trying to teach Crispin at the river?
4. Is it possible to feel the presence of a soul? How do you know you have a soul?

Chapter 26

Review Questions
1. What musical instrument did Bear teach Crispin first?
2. Why had Bear taken Crispin on?
3. What did Bear call Crispin?
4. What gift did Bear say Crispin had given the world?

Thought Questions
1. Why do you think Bear saw music to be evidence of a soul? Compare these sentiments about music to the ones discussed in *The Magician's Nephew* (Chapter 8).

Chapter 27

Review Questions
1. What did Bear see that made him uneasy? What was its cause?
2. Why did Bear ask Crispin again if he had committed the theft?
3. What did Bear decide to do instead of continuing along the road?

Thought Questions
1. What skills did Crispin need to survive? What skills are necessary for survival today?

Chapter 28

Review Questions
1. How did Bear distract Crispin from his worries?
2. What else did Crispin remember about the stranger who had come to his village?
3. What did Bear ask to see that night by the fire?

Thought Questions
1. Is it difficult to trust someone when they keep secrets from you? Explain. Compare Bear's secrecy to the ideas in *Number the Stars* and *The Hiding Place* about adults protecting children from knowledge that would be too frightening for them.

Chapter 29

Review Questions
1. What did Bear tell Crispin to do if there was ever any trouble?
2. Why was Bear going to Great Wexly on June 23?
3. Why didn't Bear fear for himself?

Thought Questions
1. Does anything truly change? Are change and freedom the same thing?
2. Do you ever fear for yourself? Why? Does making your own choices protect you from fear? If so, what kind of fear does it protect against?
3. What does the belief that innocence is more puzzling than evil tell you about Crispin and Bear's world?

Chapter 30

Review Questions
1. What village did Bear and Crispin enter? Why did they go first to the church?
2. What did Bear take from the young man in the crowd? What was his response?

3. Of what did the priest warn Bear and Crispin?
4. What news had come to the village about Lord Furnival?

Thought Questions
1. How did Bear gain the approval of the priest? Did he gain it honestly, in your opinion?

Chapter 31

Review Questions
1. Why did Crispin recognize the name of the courier?
2. What did Bear describe as a "small slip" that he had made?
3. What did Bear give Crispin from the day's work?

Thought Questions
1. What is the difference between staying alert and worrying?
2. Is there a link between freedom and the ability to earn "honest pay for honest work"? Is freedom always connected to money?

Chapter 32

Review Questions
1. Why did Bear teach Crispin how to handle a weapon?
2. Why did Crispin want to learn to make snares?
3. How did Bear picture the devil? Why?
4. What did Bear offer to make Crispin?

Thought Questions
1. What does eye contact tell you about someone?
2. Crispin's weakness, when he met Bear, was food. What is your greatest weakness?
3. How do you picture the devil? What is the basis for your mental picture? How do you think these images affect the way you think about evil?
4. Why do you think Crispin changed his mind about praying for guidance? What does that indicate about the way he was changing? Were all the changes for the better? Discuss.

Chapter 33

Review Questions
1. Describe the scene as Bear and Crispin entered Great Wexly.
2. Why did Bear give money to the Franciscan friar especially?
3. Why was the town wall built in a circle?
4. What conclusion did Crispin draw about the soldiers at the gate?

Thought Questions
1. What are big cities like today? How are the people in them similar to the crowd that Crispin saw? How are they different?
2. Why are there no walls around cities anymore? Does anything take the place of walls?

Chapter 34

Review Questions
1. What, according to Bear, was the worst disguise?
2. How did Bear and Crispin get through the gates?
3. Describe the inside of Great Wexly.
4. What did the black cloth and ribbons draped on the houses symbolize?
5. Where did Bear conduct his affairs?

Thought Questions
1. Do you prefer knowing everyone around you or knowing no one? Which makes you more uneasy? Why?
2. Is poverty relative (existing only in comparison to others) or absolute (existing even when there is nothing with which to compare)? Discuss.

Chapter 35

Review Questions
1. What did Bear tell Widow Daventry about Crispin?
2. What had happened to Lord Furnival? What was going to happen to his estate?

Thought Questions
1. What causes moments of silence in conversation? Do they make you uncomfortable? Do you think people today attach less significance to things like silence? If so, why?

Chapter 36

Review Questions
1. What room did Bear request? Why was it special?
2. What did Bear say was his real occupation?
3. What did he ask Crispin to do? What did Crispin decide to do instead?

Thought Questions
1. What did Bear mean when he said, "I'm a fool because I should like to be in Heaven before I die"? Is that possible?
2. Why did Crispin disobey Bear's orders? Do you agree with his reasons?

Chapter 37

Review Questions
1. What did Crispin do with his penny?
2. Why did Crispin enjoy not knowing where he was going?
3. Describe the woman Crispin saw. Who was she?

Thought Questions
1. When did you begin making choices? Did you find it overwhelming at first?
2. What features help you to you recognize a powerful person today?
3. Do you think people today show respect for power?

Chapter 38

Review Questions
1. What made the church so different from the building across from it?
2. Whom did Crispin see in the great cathedral?
3. What happened in the church and afterwards?

Thought Questions
1. Is it odd to think of meeting your enemy in a church? Why or why not? Are churches still thought of as safe places today?

Chapter 39

Review Questions
1. How did Crispin escape from his attackers?
2. What happened to Bear's dagger?
3. How did Crispin plan to find the city walls? Why did his plan fail at first?
4. What happened when the church bells rang?
5. How did Crispin explain Aycliffe's presence in Great Wexly?

Thought Questions
1. Has a familiar place ever become frightening to you? Did anything actually change? If not, what made it frightening? Explain.
2. What is the purpose of a curfew? Why do you think whole towns had curfews?

Chapter 40

Review Questions
1. Who yelled for Crispin to stop as he ran down the alley?
2. Whom did Widow Daventry say had arrived at the inn?
3. What did Bear sometimes forget about Crispin?

Thought Questions
1. Is ignorance an excuse for disobedience? If so, when? Defend your answer.
2. What does Bear's perseverance in coming after Crispin tell you about his character?

Chapter 41

Review Questions
1. What surprised Crispin about John Ball's identity?
2. What were Bear and Ball planning? Why did Ball think it was time to proceed?
3. What did Crispin see out in the street before he fell asleep?

Thought Questions
1. Is it always shameful to be a spy? When might that be an honorable profession?
2. What causes uprisings and revolutions? Are they always a response to injustice?

Chapter 42

Review Questions
1. Describe the inside of the Green Man Tavern.
2. Who came into the tavern? How did Crispin know him?

Thought Questions

1. Do you think there is truth to the idea of "sensing danger"? How would you explain it?
2. Avi includes many passages that vividly describe crowds of people. What do you think these descriptions add to the book as a whole? How do they create a contrast with the parts when Bear and Crispin are alone?

Chapter 43

Review Questions

1. Why did Widow Daventry send Crispin to the kitchen?
2. What did Crispin do with the broken pie?
3. What did Widow Daventry ask Crispin to do for Bear?

Thought Questions

1. How do you think Widow Daventry knew Crispin had eaten a pie? Can people tell by your face when you have done something wrong? Is guilt a good or a bad thing?

Chapter 44

Review Questions

1. Why was Bear glad to see Crispin working with the widow?
2. What were Bear's plans for leaving Great Wexly?
3. Who followed Bear when he left the Green Man Tavern?

Thought Questions

1. Why do you think Bear brushed off Crispin's concerns? Does this seem consistent with what you know of his character?
2. When and why do you think Crispin began to try to protect Bear as well as be protected by him?

Chapter 45

Review Questions

1. What kind of building did Bear enter?
2. Who followed Bear inside?
3. What did Crispin overhear? What did it mean?
4. What did Crispin see when he began to leave? Who was leading the men?

Thought Questions

1. Does it bother you to hear Bear's associates talk about dissolving the church? Why or why not? Were they actually opposed to the church? Explain.
2. Compare the declaration Ball read to the American Declaration of Independence. What similar themes do you notice?
3. The Magna Carta was confirmed in 1297, eighty years before the setting of this book. If possible, read some of this document (especially sections 1, 9, 28, and 29). How does it lay the groundwork for the rights Ball and Bear advocated?

Chapter 46

Review Questions

1. What did Crispin do when he saw the soldiers?
2. How did the rebels respond to his warning?

3. What did John Ball tell Bear just before they parted?
4. Who was captured?

Thought Questions
1. Who do you think was the soldiers' target? What makes you think that?
2. Ball told the men, "Save yourselves," so why did Bear send all the other rebels ahead of him? What do his actions tell you about his character?

Chapter 47

Review Questions
1. Where was Bear taken?
2. Why did Crispin think Bear had been taken? How did he know?
3. What happened at the Green Man Tavern when Crispin had returned to his room?

Thought Questions
1. How does reliving memories help you deal with missing someone?
2. Crispin said, "Silence was the only voice that could speak to me." Explain.

Chapter 48

Review Questions
1. What had happened to the widow?
2. What did she say would happen to Bear?
3. What did Widow Daventry advise Crispin to do?

Thought Questions
1. The widow said, "Beware all men who confuse their righteousness with the will of God." Explain. Of whom was she speaking?
2. Was Crispin at fault for what had happened? Were his small mistakes, like sneaking out to explore the city, the cause of what happened? Why or why not?

Chapter 49

Review Questions
1. What was Widow Daventry's history?
2. What did Crispin's cross say?
3. Why had Lord Furnival abandoned Crispin's mother?
4. Who was Crispin's mother? Why was Crispin in so much danger?
5. What did Widow Daventry call Crispin's death warrant?

Thought Questions
1. Does God have reasons for everything? Think carefully about your answer.
2. Does it seem odd to you that Crispin renounced his title and possible wealth so easily? Explain. What does that tell you about his values?

Chapter 50

Review Questions
1. What did the news help Crispin understand about his mother?
2. Why had Aycliffe really wanted to kill Crispin?

Thought Questions
1. Does it seem unfair that Crispin was in danger for something that wasn't his fault? Can you think of an example today in which people are judged on the basis of their relatives?
2. What did Crispin owe Bear? Did his decision to act have anything to do with his oath? Why or why not?

Chapter 51

Review Questions
1. Did the news about his family change Crispin? If so, how?
2. What did Crispin realize about the things Bear and Ball had been discussing?
3. What did he resolve to do, and why?

Thought Questions
1. Is "high blood" (or "rich blood") a blessing? Why or why not?
2. When Crispin said, "To be a Furnival was to be part of that bondage," what do you think he meant? Could he choose not to be a Furnival? Could he choose to be a Furnival and not be part of that bondage? Discuss.

Chapter 52

Review Questions
1. What news did the widow bring?
2. Where did the widow say Crispin should go?

Thought Questions
1. Would it have been right for Crispin to desert Bear, since, as the widow said, he was already lost? Was it more important for Crispin to rescue Bear or to obey Bear's order to run?

Chapter 53

Review Questions
1. Where did Crispin tell his guide to lead him?
2. What did Ball's men say when Crispin asked them for help?

Thought Questions
1. At what point would Crispin no longer have been obliged to help Bear?
2. Were Ball and the other men being practical or selfish? Is personal freedom more important than loyalty? Discuss.
3. What does torture reveal about human strength and willpower?

Chapter 54

Review Questions
1. How did Crispin get inside the palace of the Furnivals?
2. What did he take from the weapons room?

Thought Questions
1. What are some special abilities children have been given?
2. Would Crispin have been able to get inside the building at the beginning of the book? How had he changed during his time with Bear?

Chapter 55

Review Questions
1. Describe the great hall that Crispin entered.
2. What did the picture on the altar depict?
3. Who interrupted Crispin's prayer?

Thought Questions
1. Why do you think the picture of his father made Crispin angry? Can a perfect picture of someone make that person better in reality? If not, why do you think people want to create this kind of image?

Chapter 56

Review Questions
1. What did Crispin say that frightened Aycliffe? What was his proof?
2. What did Aycliffe say about Crispin's mother?
3. What did Crispin force Aycliffe to swear? What did Crispin swear?

Thought Questions
1. Why was Aycliffe afraid of Crispin? Did Crispin have something he did not?
2. Was Aycliffe right when he said, "Anyone can write words"? Why are words powerful?
3. Aycliffe said, "There's an order to things which God Himself has put in place. It can never be changed." Do you think he was misinterpreting God's order?

Chapter 57

Review Questions
1. Where did Aycliffe lead Crispin?
2. What had been done to Bear?
3. How did Crispin coerce Aycliffe into keeping his end of the bargain?

Thought Questions
1. Crispin was determined to succeed by either the dagger or the cross. What makes success by one different from success by the other?
2. Why do you think Bear was unwilling for the soldiers to touch him?

Chapter 58

Review Questions
1. What happened when they reached the city gates?
2. How did Aycliffe die?
3. What did Crispin leave on Aycliffe's chest before he left?
4. What did Bear declare about Crispin as they went down the road?

Thought Questions
1. Did Aycliffe have to die for the book to end well? Explain.
2. Why do you think Crispin left his cross behind? Is it that easy to set aside the past?
3. Bear said they had made a new truth, "In the midst of death, there is life!" Is that a new truth? Why or why not?
4. When and why do you think Crispin finally accepted his name as his true identity?

The Phantom Tollbooth
Norton Juster

Introduction

Norton Juster (1929–2021) was an architect as well as a writer. Although he dabbled in writing historical fiction, he was a master of wordplay. *The Phantom Tollbooth*, a fantasy novel, was published in 1961. The book's main character, Milo, moves from one adventure to the next as he finds the cure for boredom in learning and knowledge.

Reading Practice: Character Chart

The Phantom Tollbooth is full of characters who make only brief appearances, but whose names and personalities are puns or symbolize a bigger idea. As you read, keep a list of the people you encounter, with notes about their places of origin, roles, and relationships to each other. Include the page number with important points if possible, and keep your character chart nearby, so you can add notes and refer to it as you go.

Going Deeper: Imagery

One thing that makes Juster's writing so unique is that he takes common phrases and terms and draws attention to the strange or comical way English speakers use words every day. His use of words creates vivid pictures that incorporate all five senses.

When you read a particularly vivid passage in this book, take a minute to sketch the scene. Pay special attention to visual adjectives like color and texture, but in these cases, also look for abstract concepts, like the half-baked ideas in Chapter 7, that have been turned into something concrete. Also look for instances in which Juster has turned a sound into a color or otherwise mixed up the senses. Imagine you were responsible for designing the set and costumes for a film version of this book, and think about the ways you could bring Juster's sense of humor to life.

Chapter 1

Review Questions
1. What did Milo think was the greatest waste of time?
2. What unusual thing did Milo see in his room when he got home from school?
3. Where did Milo choose to go first?

Thought Questions
1. What does it mean to "waste" time? What in life is really worthwhile?
2. What is the "point" of learning? Does all learning have a purpose? If so, what is it?

3. Why was Milo so bored? Did he have a reason to be bored, or was it a choice? Explain.

Chapter 2

Review Questions

1. What happened when Milo drove by the tollbooth?
2. What three things did Expectations offer? Whom did Milo meet there?
3. Where did Milo end up after he took a wrong turn?
4. Who were the Lethargarians?
5. What did local ordinance 175389-J say? How was Milo breaking the law?
6. Who was the one individual in the Doldrums who didn't do nothing?
7. How did Milo get out of the Doldrums?

Thought Questions

1. How do your expectations affect the way that you experience life? Are expectations a good or bad thing?
2. Why did it rain on the Whether Man only after Milo mentioned rain? Did he cause it to rain because he expected it to?
3. Have you ever been in the doldrums? How did you get there? How did you get out?

Chapter 3

Review Questions

1. How did the watchdog get his name?
2. Why was time invented, according to Tock?
3. How did Milo get into Dictionopolis without a reason?
4. Who were the five gentlemen whom Milo met at the word market?
5. What was the main crop in Dictionopolis?
6. When did Tock say words became confusing?

Thought Questions

1. Do you think time is valuable? Why or why not?
2. How do most of the people around you treat time? Have you ever thought about time the way Tock described it, as a commodity? Can you buy and sell time? Can you own it?
3. Why is it helpful to know more than one word for the same idea?
4. Why is it important to pick your words carefully? Do skinny and slender mean the same thing? Which word would you be more likely to use? Why?
5. Are words confusing? Why or why not? Is it ever necessary to use a lot of words to say a little? If so, when?

Chapter 4

Review Questions

1. What three words did Milo want to buy in the market?
2. What kind of bee did Milo see at the "Do It Yourself" stand? How was the bee special?
3. Who was the Humbug? Were he and the bee friends?
4. Why did the bee and the Humbug start fighting? How did the fight end?

Thought Questions
1. What do Milo's three words mean? (Use a dictionary if you are unsure.) Had you heard them before? How do most people learn new words? How do you?
2. What did the "A" taste like? The "I"? The "C"? How do you think Juster chose a taste to assign to these letters? What might other letters of the alphabet taste like?
3. Why is the ability to spell important? Does the Humbug's argument about spelling make sense? Do you agree?

Chapter 5

Review Questions
1. Why did Officer Shrift accuse Milo? Of what crimes did he accuse him?
2. Whom did Milo and Tock meet in the dungeon?
3. What was the Which's role in the kingdom?
4. How did the Which fall out of favor with the king?
5. What was the only thing that could help the Which?

Thought Questions
1. What did Milo learn from his adventure in the word market?
2. Is it possible to be miserly with words? What would that look like?
3. Do you think it is worse to use too many words or too few? Why?

Chapter 6

Review Questions
1. What was the name of the kingdom the prince had founded?
2. Why had the two brothers become enemies?
3. What had the old king found when he was taking a walk?
4. Who were Rhyme and Reason?
5. Why had Azaz and the Mathemagician banished the princesses?
6. How did Milo and Tock get out of prison? Where did the king's advisors take them?

Thought Questions
1. Would it be appropriate to say evil wages war against wisdom? Discuss.
2. Can you compare words and numbers? What is the value of each?
3. What are "rhyme" and "reason"? Why are they important? Can they really "answer all problems"?

Chapter 7

Review Questions
1. What did Officer Shrift say when he saw Milo and Tock out of prison?
2. What mistake did Milo make in his speech at the banquet?
3. What is a "half-baked idea"? Give an example.

Thought Questions
1. Have you ever had to "eat your words"? If you ate them, would they taste good?
2. Can one actually taste words? Think carefully, and be prepared to explain your answer.
3. What point do you think Juster is making by assigning a taste to individual words?

Chapter 8

Review Questions
1. How did Milo convince Azaz that it would be a good idea to bring back Rhyme and Reason?
2. What did Milo have to do to bring back Rhyme and Reason?
3. What gift did King Azaz give to Milo?
4. Whom did King Azaz select to be a traveling companion for Milo and Tock?

Thought Questions
1. Can you overcome any obstacle if you know a lot of words? If not, why not?

Chapter 9

Review Questions
1. Why did the boy on the scenic route think Milo was very old?
2. What was unusual about Alec Bings? About the rest of his family?

Thought Questions
1. Do you agree with Alec's comments about point of view? Why or why not?
2. Have you ever talked to someone who had a very different point of view? Was it hard to converse?
3. If everything depends on your point of view, does that mean no one can be right or wrong? Why or why not?

Chapter 10

Review Questions
1. What was strange about the giant, the midget, the fat man, and the thin man?
2. Why didn't the man want to be ordinary?
3. Describe the city of Reality. What had happened to the city?
4. What did the orchestra play? How did the conductor lead them?
5. What happened if the orchestra stopped playing?

Thought Questions
1. Would you rather live in Illusions or Reality? What is an example today in which people pay more attention to illusions than to reality?
2. Have you ever watched a black-and-white movie? Did you like it? Is it easier to see things when they are in black-and-white or in color? Explain.
3. Juster links the sunset to an orchestra. Is there a connection between this scene and the creation of Narnia in *The Magician's Nephew*? What is the role of music in each?

Chapter 11

Review Questions
1. Why didn't Chroma direct the sunrise? How did the morning music go wrong?
2. What did Alec give Milo when they parted?
3. What kind of sounds did Dr. Dischord enjoy?
4. What was inside Dr. Dischord's bottles?
5. What was DYNNE's job?

Thought Questions
1. Can the world have too much color? What does the sunrise scene suggest about a good thing that gets out of control?
2. Do people like harsh, loud, or ugly noises? If so, why?
3. Is there a difference between silence and a lack of sound?

Chapter 12

Review Questions
1. What was wrong in the Valley of Sound?
2. Why had the Soundkeeper become angry and issued her decree?
3. What did the townspeople want Milo to do?
4. Why did the Soundkeeper collect sounds?
5. How did Milo take a sound out of the castle with him?

Thought Questions
1. What do you think a thunderclap would look like? A sneeze?
2. Is it difficult to make a sense (like hearing) experience another sense (like sight)? Why do you think Juster uses this technique in *The Phantom Tollbooth*?
3. A recurring theme in this book is people's failure to notice or appreciate beautiful things. Do you think that is true of people today?

Chapter 13

Review Questions
1. How did the Soundkeeper re-gather her extra sounds after the explosion?
2. What was the Soundkeeper's gift to Milo?
3. What happened as the three travelers drove along the beach?
4. Whom did Milo meet on the island?
5. What was the island called? How did Milo and his friends get there?
6. How did Milo and the others get off of the island?

Thought Questions
1. The Soundkeeper said, "You can't improve sound by having only silence. The problem is to use each at the proper time." How do you decide what is the proper time?
2. Why is it dangerous to jump to conclusions? How can you avoid doing it?
3. What does it mean to "swim in the Sea of Knowledge" and "come out completely dry"?

Chapter 14

Review Questions
1. What is a *dodecahedron*?
2. What was the answer to the Dodecahedron's first problem?
3. What did the Mathemagician's staff look like?
4. Was the Mathemagician angry at Milo for breaking the number? If not, why not?

Thought Questions
1. Have you ever found yourself in a situation in which you had multiple choices, but no right choice? What choice did you end up making? How did you decide?

2. In Juster's world, why do you think you must dig for numbers but words are grown?
3. Why are numbers important? Do you agree with the Dodecahedron's reasons?
4. Why didn't the people of Digitopolis value jewels? Is it natural to place value on gold and jewels? What gives them value?

Chapter 15

Review Questions
1. Why didn't the food in Digitopolis make the travelers full?
2. How did the Mathemagician travel?
3. Why was Milo disappointed when he saw the biggest number?

Thought Questions
1. The Mathemagician said, "The number you want is always at least one more than the number you've got." Why do you think people are fascinated with things that are the "biggest" or "best"? How could you apply the Mathemagician's logic to human nature?

Chapter 16

Review Questions
1. Whom did Milo meet on the stairs to Infinity?
2. Why did the child look so strange?
3. What was the only thing one could do easily, according to the Mathemagician?
4. Why hadn't Azaz answered the Mathemagician's friendly letter?
5. How did Milo convince the Mathemagician that he agreed with Azaz about something?
6. What gift did the Mathemagician give to Milo?
7. What was the first demon Milo and his friends encountered in Ignorance?

Thought Questions
1. Why is it impossible to get to infinity? Are there other characteristics of the universe that are impossible to know fully? Why do you think humans are fascinated with things they cannot understand?
2. Are averages real? Are they useful? What is the difference?
3. Milo asked, "Why is it […] that quite often even the things which are correct just don't seem to be right?" Can you answer Milo's question? How should true education distinguish between these two things?
4. Why do you think Milo had to walk rather than drive through Ignorance?

Chapter 17

Review Questions
1. Whose gift did Milo use to uncover the first demon's trick?
2. What did the "trivium" in the Terrible Trivium's name represent?
3. Did the voice that helped Milo escape belong to a good or bad character?
4. What did the second demon look like (trick question)?
5. How did Milo outwit the second demon? Whose gift did he use?
6. Why was the Gelatinous Giant ferocious? Why didn't he eat Milo and the others?

Thought Questions
1. Why, in your opinion, did the Terrible Trivium not have a face?
2. Why did the demon of insincerity help Milo escape from the Terrible Trivium? Is it possible for evil characters to have some good in them? To say things that are true?
3. Why would anyone want to protect ignorance?
4. Have you ever been angry at someone who tried to teach you? Why do you think you were angry?

Chapter 18

Review Questions
1. What did the Senses Taker use to distract Tock? Milo? The Humbug?
2. What broke the Senses Taker's spell? Why did it break the spell?
3. How did the princesses, Milo, and his friends escape from the castle?

Thought Questions
1. What is the point of laughter? Is it powerful? What does this book suggest? Do you think this book overestimates the power of laughter?
2. Reason told Milo, "You often learn more by being wrong for the right reasons than you do by being right for the wrong reasons." Explain. Do you agree?
3. What is the difference between learning for its own sake and learning for a purpose? What purposes did Reason and Rhyme suggest? What is your purpose for learning?
4. What does it mean to "build castles in the air"? Can these daydreams become a sort of prison? Discuss.

Chapter 19

Review Questions
1. Describe the demons that chased Milo away from the castle.
2. What prevented the demons from engulfing Milo and the others?
3. What was the very important thing neither Azaz nor the Mathemagician had told Milo about his quest?

Thought Questions
1. If, as the Mathemagician and Azaz told Milo, something is possible as long as you don't know that it is impossible, is "impossible" a meaningful word? Explain.
2. Why do you have to push back ignorance regularly and not just once? What does it look like for you to do that?

Chapter 20

Review Questions
1. What time was it when Milo got home? How much time had passed?
2. Why didn't Milo take another trip the next day? What had replaced the tollbooth?
3. What happened to make Milo feel more contented with staying where he was?

Thought Questions
1. What did the trip through the Phantom Tollbooth teach Milo?
2. How did Milo change by the end of the book?

3. Discuss the comment at the very end that "books [...] could take you anywhere." Do you think that is the overall message of this book? Do you agree? How does Juster's sense of humor and the style of the book turn learning into an adventure?

Looking Back, Looking Forward

Congratulations! You have now worked your way through fifteen classic works of children's literature. Along the way, you've assembled a variety of reading and thinking tools that will be valuable in future reading and writing experiences. So, you may be thinking, what now?

The Next Step

Almost every author says the key to good writing is lots and lots of reading. Good reading can start in no better place than with the classics of children's literature. If you can read these books confidently, remember key points, pick out symbolism, and compare major events and characters, you will be well on your way to writing excellent essays for high school, college, and more.

For students in the sixth to ninth grade, or for learners of any age who are ready to ask questions and think analytically about literature, a great resource for general study is *Teaching the Classics*, from The Center for Literary Education. *Teaching the Classics* guides you through a list of questions in the Socratic style that can be applied to any story, as well as a basic five-part structure for understanding works of literature.

Another resource to consider is the next book in the *Words Aptly Spoken* series, *Words Aptly Spoken®: Short Stories*. Because short stories are easy to read multiple times, they allow you to examine in detail the craft of writing an engaging story. In this guide, you'll ask similar questions about the content and style of each story (which is reprinted in full in the guide). Then, taking what you've learned from the masters of the short story form, you'll have the opportunity to stretch your imagination as you practice developing and writing your own stories.

Both of these books build on the skills you've begun to hone and will help you continue your journey through the world of literature.

Perspectives, Take Two

In today's society, mass media has an enormous impact on the way people view the world. Every day a million and one ideas compete for your attention. Most messages are designed to be absorbed passively and accepted without questioning. If nothing else, this book encourages you to practice reading (and, by default, listening and watching) with your brain fully engaged. If you can do this, you will be better prepared to distinguish between that which is merely enjoyable and that which is worthy of application to your own life.

In closing, as you continue this journey, it is worth repeating that participating in the great conversations of literature is an art that takes a lifetime to refine. However, it is an art that will yield a lifetime of fruit as you celebrate with family and friends the joy of laughing, crying, and simply bubbling over with excitement about the great stories that are now yours to share.

Best wishes on your journey!

Photo Credits

The following images have been retrieved from the Library of Congress digital Prints and Photographs collection, unless otherwise noted. The reproduction number follows the photo description.

PAGES 19 and 85:
C. S. Lewis, courtesy Encyclopedia
    Britannica, 82724-050-DE6C50B8
    CSLewis_Britannica.jpg

PAGE 25:
Elizabeth Speare, courtesy Houghton
    Mifflin Co.

PAGE 35:
Lois Lowry, courtesy Random House

PAGE 55:
Frances (Hodgson) Burnett, 1849–1924,
    LC-USZ62-77338

PAGE 123:
Avi, courtesy Harper-Collins